A New Owner's
Guide to
BEAGLES

JG-136

Overleaf: A Beagle adult and puppies. Photo by Isabelle Francais.

Opposite page: Ch. Willkeep Nicodemus owned by Denny Mounce.

The Publisher wishes to acknowledge the following owners of the dogs in this book: Steve and Candice Allmand, Valerie Barabas, Daniel Bell, Carole Bolan, Les Brandt, Branko's Beagles, Karen Byrd, Judy Formisano, Mr. and Mrs. Tom Foy, Terri Giannetti, Janet Graham, Marietta Huber, Bruce and Shirley Irwin, Joy Knapp, Londonderry Beagles, Louise Merrill, Hermann J. Mueller, Denise Nord, Lesley O'Neil, DJ Queenan, Bruce Smith, and Anita Tillman.

Photographers: Isabelle Francais, Gay Glazbrook, Marilyn Mavison, Robert Pearcy, Vince Serbin, Judith Strom, Luis F. Sosa, Karen Taylor, and Missy Yuhl.

The author acknowledges the contribution of Judy Iby for the following chapters: Sport of Purebred Dogs, Identification and Finding the Lost Dog, Traveling with Your Dog, and Health Care for Your Dog.

© T.F.H. Publications, Inc.

Distributed in the UNITED STATES to the Pet Trade by T.F.H. Publications, Inc., One T.F.H. Plaza, Neptune City, NJ 07753; distributed in the UNITED STATES to the Bookstore and Library Trade by National Book Network, Inc. 4720 Boston Way, Lanham MD 20706; in CANADA to the Pet Trade by H & L Pet Supplies Inc., 27 Kingston Crescent, Kitchener, Ontario N2B 2T6; Rolf C. Hagen Inc., 3225 Sartelon St. Laurent-Montreal Quebec H4R 1E8; in CANADA to the Book Trade by Vanwell Publishing Ltd., 1 Northrup Crescent, St. Catharines, Ontario L2M 6P5 ; in ENGLAND by T.F.H. Publications, PO Box 15, Waterlooville PO7 6BQ; in AUSTRALIA AND THE SOUTH PACIFIC by T.F.H. (Australia), Pty. Ltd., Box 149, Brookvale 2100 N.S.W., Australia; in NEW ZEALAND by Brooklands Aquarium Ltd. 5 McGiven Drive, New Plymouth, RD1 New Zealand; in Japan by T.F.H. Publications, Japan—Jiro Tsuda, 10-12-3 Ohjidai, Sakura, Chiba 285, Japan; in SOUTH AFRICA by Lopis (Pty) Ltd., P.O. Box 39127, Booysens, 2016, Johannesburg, South Africa. Published by T.F.H. Publications, Inc.
MANUFACTURED IN THE
UNITED STATES OF AMERICA
BY T.F.H. PUBLICATIONS, INC.

A NEW OWNER'S GUIDE TO
BEAGLES

HAZEL & DAVID ARNOLD

Contents

Beagles make terrific companions for young people.

Beagles are the smallest breed of English scent hounds.

Puppies must be socalized in order to blossom!

Beagles have hearty appetites and need a sound diet.

Trainable and intelligent, Beagles make fine obedience candidates.

HISTORY of the Beagle

The story of the Beagle is actually as old as time itself, tracing back through the ages to the forerunner of all dogs—*Canis lupis*, the wolf. All through the Ice Age humans were nomadic, they wandered inhospitable terrain to hunt for food. By the beginning of the Mesolithic period starting about 1200 BC, man began to make semi-permanent settlements and hunted primarily in the surrounding wooded areas for food.

Providing food for himself and his family and protecting the members of the tribe from danger was about as much as early man could handle. At that same time, however, a relationship already had begun to form between man and one of the beasts of the forests that early man was hunting— the wolf. There is little doubt that these early humans saw their own survival efforts reflected in the habits of the wolf that made ever-increasing overtures at coexistence.

The wolf families had already developed a cooperative and efficient system of hunting the food they needed for survival. Man was not only able to emulate some of these techniques, but also, as time passed, he found he was able to employ the help of the wolves themselves in capturing the animals that made up a good part of his diet. Wolves saw in man's discards a source of easily secured food, and the more cooperative wolves found they had increasingly less to fear of man. The association grew from there.

The road from wolf-in-the-wild to "man's best friend," *Canis familiaris,* is as long and as fascinating as it is fraught with widely varying explanations. The wolves that could assist man in satisfying the unending human need for food were of course most highly prized. These wolves used all their senses to hunt and capture food, and as ages passed, man realized he could selectively choose and develop certain of these senses to assist him best.

It also became increasingly obvious as the man-wolf relationship developed that certain descendants of these increasingly domesticated wolves could also be used in many survival pursuits in addition to hunting. Some of these wolves were large enough and strong enough to assist man as a beast of burden. Others were aggressive enough to protect man and the tribe he lived with from danger. In our study of the Beagle, however, it is the wolf's inherent ability to scent and pursue that is of greatest significance.

In their enlightening study of the development of the dog breeds, *The Natural History of Dogs,* authors Richard and Alice Feinnes classify most dogs as having descended from one of four major groups: the Dingo group, the Greyhound group, the Northern group and the Mastiff group. Each of these groups trace back to separate and distinct branches of the wolf family.

The Dingo group traces its origin to the Asian wolf (*Canis lupis pallipes*). Two well known examples of the Dingo group are the Basenji and, through the admixture of several European breeds, the Rhodesian Ridgeback.

A true "pack" animal, the Beagle is happiest surrounded by friends. This group of Beagles is owned by Hermann J. Mueller.

The Beagle is a dog for all seasons that can accompany his owner anywhere, regardless of the weather.

The Greyhound group descends from a coursing type relative of the Asian wolf. The group includes all those dogs that hunt by sight and are capable of great speed. The Greyhound itself, the Afghan Hound, the Borzoi and Irish Wolfhound are all examples of this group and are known as the sighthounds or coursing breeds.

The Arctic or Nordic group of dogs directly descends from the rugged northern wolf (*Canis lupis*). Included in the many breeds of this group are the Alaskan Malamute, Chow Chow, German Shepherd, and the much smaller Welsh Corgi and Spitz type dogs.

The fourth classification is the Mastiff group, which owes its primary heritage to the Tibetan wolf (*Canis lupis chanco* or *laniger*). The great diversity of the dogs included in this group indicates they are not entirely of pure blood in that the specific breeds included have undoubtedly been influenced by descendants of the other three groups.

The descendants of the Mastiff group are widely divergent but are known to include many of the scenting breeds—breeds that find game by the use of their olfactory senses rather than by sight. These breeds include those that we now classify as Sporting breeds and the true hounds. The Beagle is included in this group.

As man became more sophisticated and his lifestyle more complex he found he could produce from these descendants of the wolf dogs that could suit his specific needs. Often, these needs were based upon the manner in

Bred to locate game, the Beagle's extraordinary nose and devotion to the hunt remain constant.

which man himself went after game and the terrain in which he was forced to do so. Instead of keeping dogs that simply rounded up game and herded them toward the hunter, man was able to develop some dogs fast enough, large enough and strong enough to bring down the stag, the elk and the wild boar.

Fowl and small game had to be pursued through forests and dense undergrowth. The dense foliage could totally obscure the dog and prey, therefore a dog that kept in touch vocally with the hunter while it was in pursuit of the game was particularly useful. The Bloodhound appears to be one of the earliest breeds possessed of these talents and a good many of the scenthound breeds are descendants of the earliest Bloodhound type dogs. With the assistance of several crosses to smaller breeds, the Beagle evolved.

References to Beagle-type dogs are made in Greek writings as far back as 400 BC. The popularity of these small hounds continued on through the ages with consistent reference being made to their small size, distinctive "song" and unswerving dedication to the hunt.

The first known reference to Beagles by that name is found in the account books of Henry VIII where mention is made of payment to a Robert Shere. Shere was entrusted with the care and feeding of the King's "Begles" which "(were to) be kept sweete, wholesome and cleane."

It is not known for sure why the name Beagle was given to this breed. Some say it is a derivative of the old French word *Begueule*, which in turn owes its origins to the words *beer*, meaning to open wide, and *guele*, which meant throat. This may well have described the Beagle's deep throated call as it pursued its prey. Still others believe the name came from either the Old English *begle* or French *beigle*, both words meaning small.

The Beagle is one of the few breeds that is exceptional as a pet, show dog, field contender and hunter.

Queen Elizabeth I was another member of British royalty who fancied Beagles. Her particular favorites were the tiny variety known as "Pocket Beagles." This diminutive variety has fallen in and out of favor through the decades.

The original breed standard was written by the British Beagle Club and stated, "Pocket Beagles must not exceed 10 inches in height. Although ordinary Beagles in miniature, no point, however good in itself, should be encouraged if it tends to give a coarse appearance to such minute specimens of the breed."

By the time man's constant march to civilization had taken him through the 15th and 16th century, farmland abounded throughout Europe. What was once large forest land had been cleared and fenced. Man now was becoming accustomed to working within specified limits. The dogs he used had the hunting instincts of the great hounds of the past, but these newer hounds could be controlled by voice and horn. Rather than using just one dog to find and trail the game man was after, he used several such dogs—each to back up the other and thus avoiding mistakes and loss of the trail.

O. E. Larson's exquisite head study of a Beagle, owned by Marcia Foy.

While not always the quickest to learn their roles, these scenthounds were valued because they stubbornly refused to be diverted once on the trail. They would persist in plugging on to recapture the coldest of trails. These are characteristics which typify the scenthound of today. Often accused of being slower on the uptake than say a terrier, once the scenthound has made up his mind what the task at hand is, it is extremely difficult to dissuade the dog from his objective. This creates a special kind of persistence that must be dealt with intelligently on the part of the dog's owner.

THE BEAGLE IN ENGLAND

In England the Beagle's popularity among the royalty also earned the breed widespread interest among the nobility and sportsmen. It was not long before the average man discovered the attributes of the breed. Soon "beagling" began to nudge fox hunting out of its dominant position, if for no other reason than it was not necessary to ride behind these smaller hounds. The common man could successfully follow a Beagle pack on foot, and because the Beagle excelled as friend, companion and hunter, its popularity grew steadily throughout Great Britain and the European continent.

Author Hazel Arnold with her 13-inch Beagle Ch. Hayday Sagebrush.

The Beagle Club was formed in England in 1890 and a breed standard was drawn up at that time. The club held its first show in 1896 and shows continued to be held annually. However, interest in the breed as a show dog did not really ignite until 1931 when 27 hounds were registered with the Kennel Club and Challenge Certificates were offered at four shows.

The breed was forced to survive two World Wars during which interest and activity were minimally maintained. Upon the conclusion of World War II, activity immediately picked up and as the 50s began, championship shows and Beagle interest were at an all-time high.

It was in that period that Ch. Barvae Statute became the first Beagle to win an all-breed championship Best in Show in England. Interestingly, Statute was also sire of Ch. Derawunda Vixen, who entered the Beagle Hall of Fame by winning Best in Show at England's famed Crufts show in 1959.

THE BEAGLE IN AMERICA

The sport of beagling had rapidly gained popularity in America. It was the Beagle's ability in the field that earned the breed his notoriety. The Beagles that excelled in the field were a far cry from the attractive dogs that won prizes at shows. In all fairness, however, the field Beagle must be credited for paving the way for the breed's acceptance as a show dog in America, as it had in Great Britain and Europe.

The first Beagle to be registered with the American Kennel Club was Blunder, a pack Beagle entered into the Stud Book in 1885. Pack Beagles had prevailed in America for many years

prior to that date. Granted, one might have been hard pressed to associate them with the handsome dogs that appeared in the show rings, however. They were short of leg, long of body and lacked the bright markings typical of show dogs. They were tireless hunters, and those who owned them were unreserved in their enthusiasm for the dogs.

Following the Civil War, US General Richard Rowett imported Beagles of the finest bloodlines England had to offer at the time. These imports comprised the General's noteworthy pack of field dogs. These dogs were set apart from all others by their excellent conformation and colorful markings. It is believed that General Rowett's dogs were used as models for the first breed standard written in America in 1887, and their excellence still influences what is considered ideal to this day. That standard was drawn up by General Rowett, Dr. L.H. Twaddell and Mr. Norman Ellmore.

The National Beagle Club of America was founded in 1888 and held its first field trial for the breed two years later in Hyannis, Massachusetts. The event was noted as a success and an entry of 18 dogs was recorded.

The 20th century began with a 21-gun salute for the American Beagle as show dog. On December 21, 1901, the breed acquired its first all-breed Best in Show. The winner was Ch. Windholme's Bangle, a five-year-old female owned by Mr. Harry T. Peters. The win could not have been more appropriate in that Mr. Peters was one of the stalwarts of the breed, credited by all his many contributions to the success of the breed in America.

By 1917, popularity of the Beagle as a show dog had risen to the extent that the Westminster Kennel Club show of that

The Beagle's even temperament and sweet disposition are reasons for his continued popularity. Carolyn Anderson gives her friend Zippa a big hug.

Ch. Rock A Plenty's Wild Oats owned by Mr. and Mrs. Tom Foy, Jr. wins Best in Show at the Canadian Sportsmen's Show in 1973.

year boasted an entry of 75 dogs. Activity fluctuated through the first World War, but Beagle enthusiasts proceeded undaunted.

In 1928 Beagles were exhibited at Westminster Kennel Club's prestigious event and walked off with the Best Sporting Dog award (there was no Hound Group at that time), as well as Best Sporting Brace and Best Sporting Team in show.

It was also at the 1928 Westminster event that Beagles were first divided and shown in two separate size categories—13-inch and 15-inch. The breed has been shown in these two separate varieties ever since.

It was a Beagle, Ch. Meadowlark Draftsman, owned by Mrs. Harkness Edwards, that captured the American Kennel Club's 1939 award for top-winning American-bred dog of the year. Draftsman accomplished this honor by winning 56 Bests of Breed, 42 Hound Group One placements, and 7 Bests in Show in the 12-month period.

Interest and enthusiasm for the clever little hunter has never waned in America and Beagles have stood among the country's most popular breeds for many decades. Beagles continue to serve as wonderful companions, outstanding hunters and highly competitive showdogs from coast to coast.

CHARACTERISTICS of the Beagle

The Beagle possesses such a wealth of positive characteristics that they almost work to the breed's detriment. On the surface there appears to be so little care involved in Beagle ownership that far too many puppies are purchased without due consideration given beforehand.

The breed has undeniable appeal. In fact, if someone is still in the "deciding" stage of whether or not they should bring a Beagle puppy into their home, we strongly suggest they stay away from any home or kennel that has a litter of Beagle puppies. It is next to impossible to leave without one! Those soft brown eyes and floppy little ears make the little guys absolutely irresistible! There is nothing more captivating than a Beagle puppy!

The Beagle makes an excellent addition to the household, but make sure the entire family is ready for the responsibilities of dog ownership.

It is for this very reason that the person anticipating owning a Beagle must give serious thought to the decision. Beagle puppies are the subject for millions of picture-postcards, greeting cards and calendars each year. There is nothing more seductive than that angelic-looking little pup looking up with those soulful "won't you please adopt me?" eyes. Without a doubt—innocence personified! But in addition to being cute, Beagle puppies are living, breathing and very mischievous little creatures. They are entirely dependent upon their human owner for *everything* (and the emphasis is on *everything*) once they leave their mother and littermates.

Good breeders attempt to produce uniform litters. This Liveoak Kennel litter is certainly a splendid example of success.

Buying any dog, especially a puppy, before someone is absolutely sure he wants to make that commitment is a serious mistake. The prospective dog owner must clearly understand the amount of time and work involved in dog ownership. Failure to understand the extent of commitment dog ownership involves is one of the primary reasons so many unwanted canines end their lives in an animal shelter.

Before anyone contemplates the purchase of a dog there are some very important conditions that must be considered. One of the first important questions to be answered is whether or not the person who will ultimately be responsible for the dog's care and well being actually wants a dog.

All too often it is the mother of the household who must shoulder the responsibility of the family dog's day-to-day care. While the children in the family, perhaps even the father, may be wildly enthusiastic about having a dog, it must be remembered that they are away most of the day at school or work. It is often "mom"

How can you resist a face like this? The Beagle possesses large, soulful eyes and a "take me home" expression.

who will be taking on the additional responsibility of primary caregiver for the family dog. Somehow even the "working mom" seems to have this responsibility added to her already staggering load of duties.

Beagles love to give voice, and this young pup from Branko's Beagles obviously has something very important to say.

Pets are a wonderful method of teaching children responsibility but it should be remembered that the enthusiasm that inspires children to promise anything in order to have a new puppy may quickly wane. Who will take care of the puppy once the novelty wears off? Does that person want a dog?

Desire to own a dog aside, does the lifestyle of the family actually provide for responsible dog ownership? If the entire family is away from home from early morning to late at night, who will provide for all of a puppy's needs? Feeding, exercise, outdoor access and the like can not be provided if no one is home.

Another important factor to consider is whether or not the breed of dog is suitable for the person or the family with which it will be living. Some breeds can handle the rough and tumble play of young children, some can not. On the other hand some dogs are so large and clumsy, especially as puppies, that they could easily and unintentionally injure an infant.

Then there is the matter of hair. A luxuriously coated dog is certainly beautiful to behold, but all that hair takes a great deal of care. At first thought, it would seem therefore that a smooth-coated dog like the Beagle would eliminate this problem, but this is not so, as we will see. While there is no long hair or clipping to contend with, there is a great deal the owner of any smooth-coated dog is called upon to do in order to keep his or her companion happy and healthy.

As great as claims are for any breed's intelligence and trainability, remember the new dog must be taught every household rule that it is to observe. Some dogs catch on more quickly than others and puppies are just as inclined to forget or disregard lessons as young human children are.

A CASE FOR THE PUREBRED DOG

As previously mentioned, all puppies are cute but not all puppies grow up to be the picture of what we as humans find attractive. What is considered beauty by one person is not necessarily seen so by another. It is almost impossible to determine what a mixed breed puppy will look like as an adult. Nor is it possible to determine if the mixed breed puppy's temperament is suitable for the person or family who wishes to own it. If the puppy grows up to be too big, too stubborn or too active for the owner, what then will happen to it?

Size and temperament can vary to a degree even within a purebred breed. Still, selective breeding over many generations

In terms of grooming, the Beagle is a low-maintenance dog. The time you want to spend on grooming should be a consideration before choosing a breed.

has produced dogs giving the would-be-owner reasonable assurance of what the purebred puppy will look and act like as an adult. Points of attractiveness completely aside, this predictability is more important than one might think.

No surprises here! Purebred Beagle puppies will grow up to look like their adult relatives.

A person in training for a marathon who wants a dog to come along on those morning workouts is not going to be particularly happy with a slower-paced and short-legged breed like a Beagle. Nor will the fastidious housekeeper, whose picture of the ideal dog is one that lies quietly at the feet of his master by the hour and never sheds a hair, be particularly happy with the shaggy dog whose temperament is reminiscent of a hurricane.

Purebred puppies will grow up to look like their adult relatives and by and large they will behave pretty much like the rest of their family. Any dog, mixed breed or not, has the potential to be a loving companion. However, a purebred dog offers reasonable insurance that it will not only suit the owner's lifestyle but the person's esthetic demands as well.

WHO SHOULD OWN A BEAGLE?

What kind of a person should own a Beagle? Perhaps this question is best answered by stating first and foremost that a Beagle owner must be a person with *patience.*

If you are someone who wants a dog that lives to respond to your commands with hair-trigger speed— *forget about the Beagle!* Don't torture yourself with this breed. It isn't a case of your Beagle not understanding what you want. On the contrary, the Beagle is a very intelligent breed, but it must be understood that Beagles have a lot of interests and they may decide to pursue those interests regardless of your commands.

Do not forget the Beagle's heritage. A good Beagle never gives up the pursuit. The pursuit may be on the trail of small game or simply one of exploration. Don't expect your Beagle to change his mind or his direction easily.

A Beagle's curiosity and single-mindedness can often lead him away from home. He should be securly confined when not supervised.

A Beagle's interests and curiosity can lead him away from your home and on a course from which the dog may not easily retrace his steps. A securely fenced yard is an absolute must for the Beagle owner.

On the other hand, the Beagle is generally a very healthy dog. There is not nearly as much work involved in keeping the breed clean and healthy as with some other breeds, but this does not mean you can leave your Beagle's health to his own devices. Ears, eyes, mouth and feet need regular inspection. Even the Beagle's short coat will benefit from regular good brushings or rub downs with a rough towel.

A BREEDER CHECK LIST

Just as the buyer should have a check list to guide him or

her in locating a responsible breeder, most responsible breeders have criteria that a buyer must meet before they would be considered an ideal candidate to have one of their puppies. These are things that prospective Beagle owners should ask of themselves as well.

Security is a must—Beagles are often described as being loyal and although our egos would have us believe that our dogs would pine away if they were not with us, this is hardly the truth. A Beagle could be just as happy anywhere as long as he is fed, loved, petted and has a couch or chair to sleep on. Beagles love people and therefore they are not adverse to accepting an invitation to take a stroll

All the comforts of home! A Beagle is just as happy to be a couch potato as he is to spend the day afield.

with a passing child or hop into the car of a total stranger. For this reason the Beagle owner must have a securely fenced yard.

No home where only one of the adults is enthused about getting a Beagle— Owning a Beagle takes the cooperation of everyone in the household, and no Beagle is safe in an environment that it is not *entirely* receptive.

No home where children are solely responsible for the dog's care—Beagles are very stoic and will take almost any abuse from a child; therefore, parental supervision is an absolute must. While the best of children can love and care for their dogs, they are not always capable of understanding or remembering the special care dog ownership entails.

No home where the buyer "wants to get into breeding"—Breeding Beagles takes a great deal of time, patience and hard work. It takes a long time to understand what kind of stock is suitable for breeding and an even longer time to learn the intricacies of breeding, whelping and rearing a litter of Beagles.

STANDARD for the Beagle

Head—The skull should be fairly long, slightly domed at occiput, with cranium broad and full. *Ears*—Ears set on moderately low, long, reaching when drawn out nearly, if not quite, to the end of the nose; fine in texture, fairly broad—with almost entire absence of erectile power—setting close to the head, with the forward edge slightly inturning to the cheek—rounded at tip. *Eyes*—Eyes large, set well apart—soft and houndlike—expression gentle and pleading; of a brown or hazel color. *Muzzle*—Muzzle of medium length—straight and square-cut—the stop moderately defined. *Jaws*—Level.

Ch. BeaglesBay Midnight Serenade, owned by Vicki Phillips, winning under Michele Billings.

Lips free from flews; nostrils large and open. **Defects**—A very flat skull, narrow across the top; excess of dome, eyes small, sharp and terrierlike, or prominent and protruding; muzzle long, snipy or cut away decidedly below the eyes, or very short. Roman-nosed, or upturned, giving a dish-face expression. Ears short, set on high or with a tendency to rise above the point of origin.

Body—*Neck and Throat*—Neck rising free and light from the shoulders strong in substance yet not loaded, of medium length. The throat clean and free from folds of skin; a slight wrinkle below the angle of the jaw, however, may be allowable. **Defects**—A thick, short, cloddy neck carried on a line with the top of the shoulders. Throat showing dewlap and folds of skin to a degree termed "throatiness."

Shoulders and Chest—Shoulders sloping—clean, muscular, not heavy or loaded—conveying the idea of freedom of action with activity and strength. Chest deep and broad, but not broad enough to interfere with the free play of the shoulders. **Defects**—Straight, upright shoulders. Chest disproportionately wide or with lack of depth.

Back, Loin and Ribs—Back short, muscular and strong. Loin broad and slightly arched, and the ribs well sprung, giving

VARIETY GROUP
PLACEMENT

ANNISTON
KENNEL CLUB

SPRING 1996 ©
COPR. PHOTO BY
LUIS F. SOSA
504-889-9996

abundance of lung room. **Defects**—Very long or swayed or roached back. Flat, narrow loin. Flat ribs.

Forelegs and Feet—*Forelegs*—Straight, with plenty of bone in proportion to size of the hound. Pasterns short and straight. *Feet*—Close, round and firm. Pad full and hard. **Defects**—Out at elbows. Knees knuckled over forward, or bent backward. Forelegs crooked or Dachshundlike. Feet long, open or spreading.

Hips, Thighs, Hind Legs and Feet—Hips and thighs strong and well muscled, giving abundance of propelling power. Stifles strong and well let down. Hocks firm, symmetrical and moderately bent. Feet close and firm. **Defects**—Cowhocks, or straight hocks. Lack of muscle and propelling power. Open feet.

Tail—Set moderately high; carried gaily, but not turned forward over the back; with slight curve; short as compared with

Authors David and Hazel Arnold's 15-inch Best in Show winner Ch. Yaupon Row Sailor Boy and his 13-inch daughter Ch. Yaupon Row Polka Dot.

size of the hound; with brush. **Defects**—A long tail. Teapot curve or inclined forward from the root. Rat tail with absence of brush.

Coat—A close, hard, hound coat of medium length. **Defects**—A short, thin coat, or of a soft quality.

Color—Any true hound color.

General Appearance—A miniature Foxhound, solid and big for his inches, with the wear-and-tear look of the hound that can last in the chase and follow his quarry to the death.

SCALE OF POINTS

Head		
Skull	5	
Ears	10	
Eyes	5	
Muzzle	5	25
Body		
Neck	5	
Chest and shoulders	15	
Back, loin and ribs	15	35
Running Gear		
Forelegs	10	

Hips, thighs and hind legs	10	
Feet	10	30
Coat	5	
Stern	5	10
TOTAL	100	

Varieties—There shall be two varieties:

Thirteen Inch—which shall be for hounds not exceeding 13 inches in height.

Fifteen Inch—which shall be for hounds over 13 but not exceeding 15 inches in height.

DISQUALIFICATION

Any hound measuring more than 15 inches shall be disqualified.

Packs of Beagles

SCORE OF POINTS FOR JUDGING

Hounds—General levelness of pack	40 %
Individual merit of hounds	30 %
Total	70 %
Manners	20 %
Appointments	10 %
TOTAL	100 %

Levelness of Pack—The first thing in a pack to be considered is that they present a unified appearance. The hounds must be as near to the same height, weight, conformation and color as possible.

The versatile Beagle can excel at many different activities, including agility. Rio, owned by Lesley O'Neil, conquers the tire jump with ease.

Individual Merit of the Hounds—Is the individual bench-show quality of the hounds. A very level and sporty pack can be gotten together and not a single hound be a good Beagle. This is to be avoided.

Manners—The hounds must all work gaily and cheerfully, with flags up—obeying all commands cheerfully. They should be broken to heel up, kennel up, follow promptly

Ch. Liveoak Honky Tonk Hero, CD owned by Steve and Candice Allmand, is believed to be the only Beagle to stand among the top five of his breed in both obedience and conformation competition.

and stand. Cringing, sulking, lying down to be avoided. Also, a pack must not work as though in terror of master and whips. In Beagle packs it is recommended that the whip be used as little as possible.

Appointments—Master and whips should be dressed alike, the master or huntsman to carry horn—the whips and master to carry light thong whips. One whip should carry extra couplings on shoulder strap.

RECOMMENDATIONS FOR SHOW LIVERY

Black velvet cap, white stock, green coat, white breeches or knickerbockers, green or black stockings, white spats, black or dark brown shoes. Vest and gloves optional. Ladies should turn out exactly the same except for a white skirt instead of white breeches.

Approved September 10, 1957

SELECTING the Right Beagle For You

The Beagle puppy you bring into your home will be your best friend and a member of your family for many years to come. The average well–bred and well–cared–for Beagle is apt to live far longer than a good many of the large breeds. A Beagle can easily live to be 14, 16 or even 17 years old.

Early care and sound breeding is vital to the longevity of your Beagle. Therefore it is of the utmost importance that the dog you select has had every opportunity to begin life in a healthy, stable environment and comes from stock that is both physically and temperamentally sound.

The only way you can be assured of all this is to go directly to a breeder who has consistently produced Beagles of this kind over the years. A breeder earns his or her reputation through a well-planned breeding program that has been governed by rigid selectivity.

A two-week-old tricolor Beagle puppy is hardly more than a handful for breeder Candice Allmand.

Selective breeding programs are aimed at maintaining the breed's many fine qualities and keeping the breed free of as many genetic weaknesses as possible.

Anyone who has ever bred dogs will quickly tell you this selective process is both time consuming and costly for a breeder and that no one ever makes money breeding sound and healthy dogs. One of the many things it does accomplish, however, is to ensure you of getting a Beagle that will be a joy to own. Responsible Beagle breeders protect their tremendous investment of time and money by basing their breeding programs on the healthiest, most representative breeding stock available. These breeders provide each following generation with the very best care, sanitation and nutrition available.

Londonderry's True Love's Abby demonstrates the Beagle's talent for getting into all kinds of situations.

Governing kennel clubs in the different countries of the world maintain lists of local breed clubs and breeders that can lead a prospective Beagle buyer to responsible breeders of quality stock. If you are not sure of where to contact an established breeder in your area, we strongly recommend getting in touch with your local or national kennel club for recommendations.

There is little doubt that you will be able to find an established Beagle breeder in your own area. Finding a local breeder will allow you to visit the breeder's home or kennel, inspect the facility and, in many cases, see a puppy's parents and other relatives. Good breeders are always willing and able to discuss any problems that might exist in the breed and how they should be dealt with.

If there aren't any Beagle breeders in your immediate area, rest assured taking the time and exerting the effort to plan a trip to a reputable breeder's home or kennel will be well worth your while. If this is not possible, some breeders will arrange to ship a puppy to you by air. The shipping details are best discussed with the breeder.

Never hesitate to ask the breeder you visit or speak to on the phone any questions or concerns you might have relative to Beagle ownership. As you have already noted, responsible breeders ask many questions of those who anticipate purchasing a puppy from them. Expect any Beagle breeder to ask these and perhaps even more questions as well. Good breeders are just as interested in placing their Beagle puppies in a loving and safe environment as you are in obtaining a happy, healthy puppy.

Not all good breeders maintain large kennels. In fact, you are just as apt to find quality Beagles from the homes of small hobby breeders who keep only a few dogs and have litters only occasionally. The names of these people are just as likely to appear on the recommended lists from kennel clubs as are the larger kennels which maintain many dogs. Hobby breeders are equally dedicated to breeding quality dogs. A factor in favor of the hobby breeder is the distinct advantage of being able to raise puppies in a home environment with all the accompanying personal attention and socialization.

Again, it is important that both the buyer and the seller ask questions. Be extremely suspicious of anyone who is willing to sell you a Beagle puppy with no questions asked.

Do not just show up on the doorstep of a breeder's home or kennel. Call ahead and make an appointment at a convenient time so that you will be expected and not rushed.

A proud mom from Londonderry Kennels has her one-week-old pups all lined up and ready for inspection.

Recognizing a Healthy Puppy

Beagle breeders seldom release their puppies until the puppies are at least eight weeks of age and have been given at least one of their puppy inoculations. By the time the litter is eight weeks, the puppies are entirely weaned and no longer nursing on the mother. While puppies are nursing

The puppy you choose should be bright-eyed, alert and healthy looking. Louise Merrill's identically marked tricolor trio all fit the bill.

As highly titled as they might be, Taylor (Teloca Fire And Rain, TD) and Rio (U-CD Teloca Miami Sound Machine, CD, TD, CGC, ASCA, CD) are also simply sweet, loving Beagles.

they have a degree of immunity from their mother. Once they have stopped nursing they become highly susceptible to many infectious diseases. A number of these diseases can be transmitted

on the hands and clothing of humans, therefore it is extremely important that your puppy is current on all the shots he must have for his age.

A healthy Beagle puppy is a happy, tail-wagging extrovert. Personalities and temperaments within a litter can range from very active to completely passive. Some puppies are ready to play with the world, others simply want to crawl up into your lap and be held. While you should never select a puppy that appears shy or listless because you feel sorry for him, we would not hesitate to select the puppy that is calm and quiet, just as long as he is healthy.

Taking a puppy that appears sickly and needy will undoubtedly lead to heartache and expensive veterinary costs. Do not attempt to make up for what the breeder did not do in providing proper care and nutrition. It seldom works.

If at all possible take the Beagle puppy you are attracted to into a different room in the kennel or house in which he was raised. The smells will remain the same for the puppy so he should still feel secure, and this will give you an opportunity to see how the puppy acts away from his littermates, as well as give you an opportunity to inspect the puppy more closely.

Above all, the puppy should be clean. The skin should be pliable and the coat smooth and soft. The inside of a healthy puppy's ears will be pink and clean. Dark discharge or a bad odor could indicate ear mites, a sure sign of lack of cleanliness and poor maintenance. A Beagle puppy's breath should always smell sweet. The nose of a healthy puppy is cold and wet and there should be no discharge of any kind.

There should never be any malformation of the jaw, lips or nostrils. Make sure there is no rupture of the navel.

The puppy's teeth must be clean and bright and the eyes should be dark and clear. Runny eyes or eyes that appear red and irritated could be caused by a myriad of problems, none of which indicate a healthy puppy. Coughing or diarrhea are absolute danger signals.

A Beagle puppy's movement should be free and easy and he should never express any difficulty in moving about. Sound conformation can be determined even at eight or ten weeks of age.

The puppy's attitude tells you a great deal about his state of health. Puppies that are feeling "out of sorts" react very quickly and will usually find a warm littermate to snuggle up to and prefer to stay that way even when the rest of the "gang" wants to play or go exploring.

VARIETIES

There are two varieties of Beagle, those that in adulthood do not exceed 13 inches and those that are at least 13 but do not exceed 15 inches. The height is measured at the withers (top of shoulder). While these measurements mean little to the pet owner, a Beagle that measures over 15 inches is subject to disqualification and may not be shown.

MALE OR FEMALE?

The sex of a dog in many breeds is an important consideration, and of course there are sex-related differences in the Beagle that the prospective buyer should consider. In the end, however, the assets and liabilities of each sex do balance each other out and the final choice remains with the individual preference.

Well-cared-for Beagles can live much longer than many other breeds. Many veterans are sound and healthy to 17 years of age.

The male Beagle makes just as loving and devoted a companion as the female. He can of course be a bit more headstrong as an adolescent, and this will require a bit more patience on the part of his owner. Here again, the owner's dedication to persistence in training will determine the final outcome.

Male dogs of most breeds have a natural instinct to lift their leg and urinate to "mark" their home territory. It seems confusing to many dog owners, but a male marking his home turf has absolutely nothing to do with whether or not he is housebroken. The two responses come from entirely different needs and must be dealt with in that manner. Some dogs are more difficult to train not to mark within the confines of the household than others. Males that are used for breeding are even more prone to this response and are even harder to break of it.

Females have semi-annual "heat" cycles once they have reached sexual maturity. These cycles usually occur for the first time at about nine or ten months of age and last about 21 days. They are accompanied by a bloody vaginal discharge for a part of that time. The discharge creates the need to confine the female to an area where she will not soil furniture or carpeting. There are also "pants" that can be obtained from your pet shop that will help avoid her "spotting" the area in which she lives. It must be understood that the female has no control over this bloody discharge so it has nothing to do with training.

Confinement of the female in heat is especially important to prevent unwanted attention from some neighborhood Lothario or she may become pregnant. Even a moment or two alone can result in an unwanted litter of mongrel puppies.

These sexually related problems can be eliminated by spaying the female and neutering of the male. Unless a Beagle is purchased expressly for breeding or showing from a breeder capable of making this judgment, your pet should be sexually altered.

Breeding and raising Beagles should be left in the hands of people who have the facilities and knowledge to do the job properly. Only those who have the facilities to keep each and every puppy they breed until the correct home is found for him should ever contemplate raising a litter. This can often take many months after a litter is born. Most single dog owners are not equipped to this.

Naturally a responsible dog owner would never allow his or her pet to roam the streets and end his life in an animal shelter. Unfortunately, being forced to place a puppy due to space constraints before you are able to thoroughly check out the prospective buyer may in fact create this exact situation.

Parents will often ask to buy a female "just as a pet" but with full intentions of breeding so that their children can witness "the miracle of birth." There are countless books and videos now available which portray this wonderful event. Altering one's companion dogs eliminates bothersome household problems and precautions.

It should be understood, however, that spaying or neutering are not reversible procedures. Spayed females or neutered males are not allowed to be shown in conformation shows of most countries, nor will altered animals ever be able to be used for breeding.

SELECTING A SHOW PROSPECT PUPPY

If you or your family are considering a show career for your puppy we strongly advise putting yourself in the hands of an established breeder who has earned a reputation for breeding winning show dogs. They and they alone are most capable of anticipating what one might expect a young puppy of their line to develop into when it reaches maturity.

Although the potential buyer should read the official standard of perfection for the Beagle, it is hard for the novice to really understand the nuances of what is being asked for. The experienced breeder is best equipped to do so and will be only too happy to assist you in your quest. Even at that, no

This young Whisperfield Beagle is an excellent example of what the standard calls for in substance and balance.

one can make accurate predictions or guarantees on a very young puppy.

Any predictions a breeder is apt to make are based upon his or her experience with past litters that produced winning showdogs. It should be obvious the more successful a breeder has been in producing winning Beagles through the years, the broader his basis of comparison will be. "Quality begets quality" is an old stockman's adage that certainly applies in this instance.

The most any responsible breeder will say about an eight-week-old puppy is that it has "show potential." If you are serious about showing your Beagle most breeders strongly suggest waiting until a puppy is at least four or five months old before making any decisions.

The standard has a very detailed description of how a top-quality Beagle should look and how he should move. Some things even the complete novice can determine, other things take an expert's eye, and even they are educated guesses when evaluating puppies.

Many breeders believe the ideal time to select a show prospect Beagle puppy is 12 weeks of age. At this time puppies reflect in a very large part what they will look like as adults.

The show puppy should have a short-coupled "cobby" body with overall substance, good bone and muscle development. Even the smallest Beagle should have good substance for his size. The show Beagle should never look overly refined or spindly. Evaluating movement, however, is something that takes the experienced person's opinion.

The Beagle's expression is soft and hound-like, often described as loving and gentle. Eyes are large and kind, brown or hazel in color.

The Beagle carries his tail gaily, that is, perpendicularly to his back. It may curve very slightly forward toward the dog's

Even if a puppy possesses physical faults, it will not stop him from being a wonderful pet. Londonderry's Melissa Sue and Woody share an important secret.

These two eight-week-old puppies bred by Candice Allmand grew up to be real champs—one in the show ring and one in the household.

head but it should never bend forward from the root.

Should you be totally committed to buying a Beagle of one size or the other, buy an adult dog. It is absolutely impossible to predict ultimate size in a young puppy! Experienced breeders can make educated guesses but they are just that— *guesses.* Just because a Beagle is of a particular size does not restrict her to producing only that size. All Beagles are capable of producing 13- or 15-inch offspring.

There are many "beauty point" shortcomings a Beagle puppy might have that would in no way interfere with him being a wonderful companion. At the same time these faults could be serious drawbacks in the show ring. Many of these faults are such that a beginner in the breed might hardly notice. This is why employing the assistance of a good breeder is so important. Still, the prospective buyer should be at least generally aware of what the Beagle show puppy should look like and know what faults would bar him from being a winner in the show ring.

All of the foregoing regarding soundness and health in selecting a companion puppy apply to the show puppy as well. The show prospect must be sound, healthy and adhere to the standard of the breed very closely.

The complete AKC standard of the Beagle appears in this book and can assist the newcomer to learn more about the Beagle. The more you know about the history and development of the breed, the better equipped you will be to see the differences that distinguish the show dog from the pet.

If you do not have the time or inclination to train a puppy, consider adopting an adult Beagle.

The things that really define a show prospect puppy are type, balance and temperament—three simple words that have so many nuances it takes most breeders an entire lifetime to fully comprehend even a good part of them.

Type: Type includes the characteristics that differentiate the breed from all other purebred breeds. Paramount among these features of course are the Beagle's warm and appealing expression, small size and long ears. The beautiful hound coloring and small size also help establish this as a Beagle and not some other breed.

Balance: Balance is the manner that all the desirable characteristics fit together. Their combination creates the picture of quality that says "I am the best Beagle that ever was!" For instance, the Beagle puppy's back is short and level without a dip or roach and it connects the puppy's two ends in such a manner that the youngster moves with ease.

Temperament: The correct Beagle temperament combines all the wonderful characteristics that make him such a beloved companion. In the show ring the Beagle is a happy and determined performer— a dog that moves about with a casual air and love of life.

Ch. White Acres Merry Paige owned by authors David and Hazel Arnold.

PUPPY OR ADULT?

For the person anticipating a show career for their Beagle or for someone hoping to become a breeder, the purchase of a young adult provides greater certainty with respect to quality. Even those who simply want a companion could consider the adult dog.

In some instances breeders will have males or females they no longer wish to use for breeding or that have developed some show ring flaw that diminishes their chances for a successful show career. Also on occasion a Beagle is returned to the breeder because the owner moves or is no longer able to keep a dog.

Beagles of this kind could make a wonderful companion for someone, and acquiring an adult dog eliminates the many problems raising a puppy involves. Beagles are a breed that can "transfer" well, provided they are given the affection and attention they need.

Elderly people often prefer the adult dog, particularly one that is housebroken. The adult dog can be easier to manage, requiring less supervision and damage control. Adult Beagles are seldom "chewers" and are usually more than ready to adapt to household rules.

There are things to consider though. Adult dogs have usually developed behaviors that may or

There is no limit to the mischief a baby Beagle can get into. These two Londonderry pups are off to fix the plumbing!

No matter what age Beagle you own, the loyalty and devotion your Beagle displays will remain constant. may not fit into your routine. If an adult Beagle has never been housebroken or has never been exposed to small children it will obviously take some very concentrated effort on the part of the new owner to compensate for these shortcomings.

Children are also inclined to be more active and vocal than the average adult, and this could intimidate the dog as well. Properly introduced and supervised, however, the relationship between a Beagle and a child will usually develop quickly and beautifully.

We strongly advise taking an adult Beagle on a trial basis to see if the dog will adapt to the new owner's lifestyle and environment. Most often it works, but on rare occasions a prospective owner decides training his or her dog from puppyhood is worth the time and effort required.

IMPORTANT PAPERS

The purchase of any purebred dog entitles you to three very important documents: a health record which includes a list of inoculations, a copy of the dog's pedigree and a registration certificate.

Health and Inoculation Records: You will find that most Beagle breeders have initiated the necessary preliminary inoculation series for their puppies by the time they are eight weeks of age. These inoculations temporarily protect the puppies against hepatitis, leptospirosis, distemper and canine parvovirus. "Permanent" inoculations will follow at a prescribed time. Because breeders and veterinarians follow different approaches to inoculations, it is important that the health record you obtain for your puppy accurately lists which shots have been given and when. In this way the veterinarian you choose will be able to continue on with the appropriate inoculation series as needed. In most cases rabies inoculations are not given until a puppy is three months of age or older.

The breeder will have started your Beagle pup on the road to good nutrition, so stick to this original diet.

Pedigree: The pedigree is your Beagle's "family tree." The breeder must supply you with a copy of this document authenticating your puppy's ancestors back to at least the third generation. All purebred dogs have pedigrees. The pedigree in itself does not mean that your puppy is of show quality. All it means is that all of his ancestors were in fact registered Beagles. They may all have been of pet quality.

Unscrupulous puppy dealers often try to imply that a pedigree indicates that all dogs having one are of

Reputable breeders will provide you with all the necessary documents when you take home your Beagle pup. A quintet of Starcrest Beagles with their breeder Hermann Mueller.

championship caliber. This is not true. Again, a pedigree simply tells you all of the dog's ancestors are purebred.

Registration certificate: A registration certificate is the canine world's "birth certificate." This certificate is issued by a country's governing kennel club. When the ownership of your Beagle is transferred from the breeder's name to your name, the transaction is entered on this certificate and, once mailed to the appropriate kennel club, it is permanently recorded in their computerized files.

Keep all of your dog's documents in a safe place as you will need them when you visit your veterinarian or should you ever wish to breed or show your Beagle. Keep the name, address and phone number of the breeder from whom you purchase your dog in a separate place as well. Should you ever lose any of these important documents, you will then be able to contact the breeder regarding obtaining duplicates

DIET SHEET

When you bring your Beagle home for the first time, he should be a happy and healthy little extrovert. This is due in a good part to the care and feeding he received from the breeder. Every breeder we know has their own particular way of feeding. Most breeders give the new owner a written record that details the amount and kind of food a puppy has been receiving. Follow these recommendations to the letter at least for the first month or two after the puppy comes to live with you.

The diet sheet should indicate the kinds of food and number of times a day your Beagle puppy has been accustomed to being fed. The kinds of vitamin supplementation, if any, the puppy has been receiving is also important. Following the prescribed procedure will reduce the chance of upset stomach and loose stools.

Usually a breeder's diet sheet projects the increases and changes in food that will be necessary as your puppy grows from week to week. If the sheet does not include this information, ask the breeder for suggestions regarding increases and the eventual changeover to adult food.

In the unlikely event you are not supplied with a diet sheet by the breeder and are unable to get one, your veterinarian will be able to advise you in this respect. There are countless foods now being manufactured expressly to meet the nutritional needs of puppies and growing dogs. A trip down the pet aisle at your supermarket will prove just how many choices there are. Two important tips to remember: read labels carefully for content, and established, reliable manufacturers are more likely to give you what you pay for.

HEALTH GUARANTEE

Any reputable breeder is more than willing to supply a written agreement that the purchase of your Beagle is contingent upon his passing a veterinarian's examination. Ideally you will be able to arrange an appointment with your chosen veterinarian right after you have picked up your puppy from the breeder and before you take the puppy home. If this is not possible you should not delay this procedure any longer than 24 hours from the time the puppy leaves the breeder's home.

TEMPERAMENT AND SOCIALIZATION

Temperament is both hereditary and learned. Inherited good temperament can be ruined by poor treatment and lack of proper socialization. A Beagle puppy which comes from shy or nervous stock is a poor risk to serve his owner in any capacity. A shy puppy would certainly not fare well in the field nor would it make a pleasant companion or winning showdog. An unstable Beagle should never be bred. Therefore it is critical that you obtain a happy puppy from a breeder who is determined to produce good temperaments and has taken all the necessary steps early on to provide the early socialization necessary.

It is important that your Beagle pup meet as many different people as possible—especially children. This well-socialized pup gives his friend a big kiss!

Taking your puppy to "puppy kindergarten" class is one of the best things you can do for him. There he will learn how to obey basic training commands as well as how to interact with other dogs and people.

Temperaments in the same litter can range from confident and outgoing on the high end of the scale to shy and fearful at the low end. By and large, however, Beagle temperament is and should be confident and friendly.

If you are fortunate enough to have children in the household or living nearby, your socialization task will be assisted considerably. Beagles raised with well supervised children are the best. The two seem to understand each other and in some way known only to the puppies and children themselves, they give each other the confidence to face the trying ordeal of growing up.

The children in your own household are not the only children your puppy should spend time with. It is a case of the more the merrier! Every child (and adult for that matter) that enters your household should be introduced to your Beagle. If trustworthy neighbor children live nearby, have them come in and spend time with your puppy if there is adult supervision. The children must understand, however, that puppies are babies and cannot endure rough handling, nor can they play for hours on end without rest periods.

Weather permitting, your puppy should go everywhere with you: the post office, the market, to the shopping mall— wherever. Be prepared to create a stir wherever you go because the very reason that attracted you to the first Beagle you met applies to other people as well. Everyone will want to pet your little cherub and there is nothing in the world better for him.

An important note, however— *do not leave your Beagle alone in a car during hot or even warm weather!* Temperatures inside a closed car can soar in just a few minutes and this could cause the death of your dog.

The young Beagle will quickly learn all humans— young and old, short and tall, and of all races—are friends. You are in charge. You must call the shots.

If your Beagle has a show career in his future, there are other things in addition to just being handled that will have to be taught. All show dogs regardless of breed must learn to have their mouth inspected by the judge. The judge must also be able to check the teeth. Males must be accustomed to having their testicles touched as the dog show judge must determine that all male dogs are "complete." This means there are two normal sized testicles in the scrotum. These inspections must begin in puppyhood and be done on a regular and continuing basis.

THE ADOLESCENT BEAGLE

Beagles go through growth periods in "spurts." Parts of the anatomy seem to develop independently of each other. One day your puppy will have a straight and firm back. The next day it will appear to sag and the day after that it may look like a camel's hump. Despair not. Eventually, *eventually*, your Beagle will almost always revert back to what he gave promise of being as a puppy.

If your Beagle begins to emit an odor, check inside those long ears. Because of lack of air circulation inside the ear, the opening to the ear canal can be a place to harbor ear mites or where infections start. It may be necessary for your veterinarian to use a swab and do a microscopic examination of the residue inside your dog's ears in order to determine what the problem is.

Food requirements will change during this growth period. Think of Beagle puppies as individualistic as children and act accordingly.

The amount of food you give your Beagle should be adjusted to how much he will consume at each meal and how that amount relates to optimum weight. Healthy Beagles have ravenous appetites and will eat far more than they need to stay fit. You must be extremely careful not to let them get too fat.

Beagles can give you a forlorn look that says they are at starvation's doorstep regardless of how much food you give them. Excess weight for Beagles (or their owners for that matter!) can be lethal. If the entire meal is eaten quickly, add a small amount to the next feeding and continue to do so as the need increases. This method will ensure you of

Who knows what lies ahead for your Beagle pup? This sweet little guy grew up to be Can. Am. Ch. Ebbtide Whisperfield Able.

giving your puppy enough food, but you must also pay close attention to your dog's appearance.

At eight weeks of age, a Beagle puppy is eating four meals a day. By the time he is six months old, the puppy can do well on two meals a day with perhaps a snack in the middle of the day. If a Beagle puppy does not eat the food offered, he is either not hungry or not well. A healthy Beagle will always eat when he is hungry. If you suspect the dog is not well, a trip to the veterinarian is in order.

Your Beagle will have to learn to conform to the rules of the household in order to become a valued family member.

Beagles are hounds and have an inbred howling mechanism that they do not hesitate to use—especially when left "home alone." Constant correction and not permitting your young Beagle to become accustomed to howling away in your absence will certainly be appreciated by your neighbors!

Another hound characteristic is the Beagle's trailing ability. The breed is constantly checking the ground for interesting odors to follow and if not kept in a fenced yard will more likely than not end the day's trailing several counties away. While they are excellent trailers, Beagles are not blessed with the "homing" instinct of some other breeds. Responsible owners make sure their Beagle is kept in a safe and secure environment and that he has a collar with identification tags securely attached at all times.

This adolescent period is a particularly important one as it is the time your Beagle must learn all the household and social rules by which he will live for the rest of his life. Your patience and commitment during this time will not only produce a respected canine good citizen, but will forge a bond between the two of you that will grow and ripen into a wonderful relationship.

When properly introduced, a well-socialized Beagle will get along with anybody—or anything! This Branko Beagle has made a feline friend.

CARING for Your Beagle

FEEDING AND NUTRITION

Following the diet sheet provided by the breeder from whom you obtain your Beagle puppy is the best way to make sure the puppy gets the right amount and the correct type of food for his age. Do your best not to change the puppy's diet and you will be less apt to run into digestive problems and diarrhea. Diarrhea is very serious in young puppies. Puppies with diarrhea can dehydrate very rapidly causing severe problems and even death.

If it is necessary to change your Beagle puppy's diet for any reason it should be done gradually, over a period of several meals and a few days. Begin by adding a tablespoon or two of the new food and gradually increase the amount until the meal consists entirely of the new product.

At about six months of age the Beagle puppy can do well on three meals a day— morning, noon and night. By the time your Beagle is 10 to 12 months old, you can reduce feedings to one or at the most two a day. The main meal can be given either in the morning or evening. It is really a matter of choice on your part. There are two important things to remember: feed the main meal or meals at the same time every day and make sure what you feed is nutritionally complete.

The single meal can be supplemented by a morning or night time snack of hard dog biscuits made especially for medium or

Choose a brand of dog food that is nutritious and specially formulated for your Beagle's stage of life.

large dogs. The largest size biscuits are particularly good for a Beagle's teeth and gums but if the dog finds them too much to handle, the medium size biscuits will do nearly as well.

"BALANCED" DIETS

In order for a canine diet to qualify as "complete and balanced" in the United States, it must meet standards set by the Subcommittee on Canine Nutrition of the National Research Council of the National Academy of Sciences.

Treats can be given to your Beagle, but make sure they are healthy and do not upset his regular diet.

Beagles love "people food," but diving into the Easter candy is definitely a bad idea.

Most commercial foods manufactured for dogs meet these standards and prove this by listing the ingredients contained in the food on every package or can. The ingredients are listed in descending order with the main ingredient listed first.

Fed with any regularity at all, refined sugars can quickly cause your Beagle to become obese and will definitely create tooth decay. Candy stores do not exist in nature and canine teeth are not genetically disposed to handling sugars. Do not feed your Beagle candy or sweets and avoid products that contain sugar to any high degree.

Fresh water and a properly prepared, balanced diet containing the essential nutrients in correct proportions are all a healthy Beagle needs to be offered. Dog foods come canned, dry, semi-moist, "scientifically fortified" and "all-natural." A visit to your local supermarket or pet store will reveal how vast an array you will be able to select from.

Newborn puppies get the nutrients they need from nursing, but once you bring your Beagle home, you are responsible for providing him with the proper diet.

All dogs, from toy to giant-sized, are carnivorous (meat-eating) animals, and the basis of the diet they are fed should be animal protein. The product can be canned or dried, but check ingredients to make sure that the major ingredient (appearing first on the ingredients list) is in fact animal protein.

Wild carnivores eat the entire beast they capture and kill. The carnivore's kills consist almost entirely of herbivores (plant eating) animals and invariably the carnivore begins his meal with the contents of the herbivore's stomach. This provides the carbohydrates, minerals and nutrients present in vegetables.

Your Beagle's food intake will need to be increased during his growth periods. First, this little guy needs to grow into his bowl!

Through centuries of domestication we have made our dogs entirely dependent upon us for their well being. Therefore we are entirely responsible for duplicating the food balance the wild dog finds in nature. The domesticated dog's diet must include some protein, carbohydrates, fats, roughage and small amounts of essential minerals and vitamins.

Finding commercially prepared diets that according to the label contain all the necessary nutrients in the proper balance will not present a problem. It is important to understand, however, that these commercially prepared foods do contain a high concentration of the nutrients your Beagle requires. While a good many Beagle breeders recommend some vitamin supplementation for a healthy coat and increased stamina, especially for show dogs, pregnant bitches or growing puppies, it is important that discretion be used.

OVER-SUPPLEMENTATION

A great deal of controversy exists today regarding the orthopedic problems which afflict many breeds. Some claim these problems are entirely hereditary conditions but many others feel they can be exacerbated by over-use of mineral and vitamin supplements for puppies. Over-supplementation is now looked upon by some breeders as a major contributor to many skeletal abnormalities found in the purebred dogs of the day. In giving vitamin supplementation one should *never* exceed the prescribed amount. No vitamin, however, is a substitute for a nutritious, balanced diet.

POPpups™ by Nylabone® are 100% edible and enhanced with dog-friendly ingredients like liver, cheese, spinach, chicken, carrots or potatoes. They contain no salt, sugar, alcohol, plastic or preservatives. You can even microwave a POPpup™ to turn it into a huge crackly treat.

There is a growing trend among breeders to cook their dogs' food "from scratch," combining their own special mixture of vegetables and animal protein. In doing so they eliminate the preservatives from their dogs' diets that are found in many commercially prepared foods. It is very important to discuss this feeding method with your veterinarian so that you are sure to include all the necessary nutrients your dog requires.

Pregnant and lactating bitches do require supplementation of some kind, but here again it is not a case of "if a little is good, a lot would be a great deal better." Extreme caution is advised in this case and the use of these supplementations is best discussed with the breeder from whom you purchased your Beagle or your veterinarian.

If you put your Beagle on a regular feeding schedule, he will always know when its time to eat.

Table scraps should be given only as part of the dog's meal and never from the table. A Beagle that becomes accustomed to being hand fed from the table can become a real pest at meal time very quickly. Also dinner guests may find the woeful and pleading stare of your Beagle is less than appealing when dinner is being served.

Dogs do not care if food looks like a hot dog or a piece of cheese. Truly nutritious dog foods are seldom manufactured to look like food that appeals to humans. Dogs only care about how food smells and tastes. It is highly doubtful you will be eating your dog's food, so do not waste your money on these "looks just like" products.

SPECIAL DIETS

There are now any number of commercially prepared diets for dogs with special dietary needs. The overweight, underweight or geriatric dog can have his nutritional needs met, as can puppies and growing dogs. The calorie content of these foods is adjusted accordingly. With the correct amount of the right foods and the proper amount of exercise, your Beagle should stay in top shape. Again, common sense must prevail. Too many calories and too little exercise will increase weight. Increasing the amount of exercise and reducing the number of calories will reduce weight. It is as simple as that.

A young Beagle going through the teething period may become a poor eater. The concerned owner's first response is to tempt the dog by hand-feeding special treats and foods which the problem eater seems to prefer. This practice only serves to compound the problem. Once the dog learns to play the waiting game, he will turn up his nose at anything other than his favorite food, knowing full well what he *wants* to eat will eventually arrive.

Unlike humans, dogs have no suicidal tendencies. A healthy dog will not starve himself to death. He may not eat enough to keep him in the shape we find ideal and attractive, but he will definitely eat enough to maintain himself. If your Beagle is not eating properly and appears to be too thin, it is probably best to consult your veterinarian; however, finicky eaters are rare among Beagles.

These two Whisperfield puppies have no difficulty sharing their treats with a German Shorthaired Pointer friend.

Yard work is hard work! Two Liveoak Kennel pups have had their fill of exercise and take a midday snooze after tending their ·garden.

Exercising

Within reason, most anything you can do, your Beagle can do too. Long morning walks, hikes over mountain trails, exploring tide pools along the beach— your Beagle will enjoy and benefit from these activities as much as you will.

On the other hand, if your own exercise proclivities lie closer to a good long walk around the shopping mall, your Beagle can be just as satisfied. The Beagle has an outstanding level of endurance but he is not one that has to be worn down before he will lie down.

If there are young children or other dogs or cats in your household, your Beagle could already be getting enough exercise. Even at that, the Beagle is always ready for a romp or ready to invent some new game or participate in one that his best pal or kennel mate might invent.

The Beagle is a very athletic dog and enjoys regular exercise. Bonny Sunshine Sara UKC, CD, owned by Joy Knapp sails over a jump in an obedience trial.

Slow, steady exercise that keeps the heart rate in the working area will do nothing but extend your dog's life. If your Beagle is doing all this with you at his side, you are increasing the chances that the two of you will enjoy each other's company for many years to come.

Toys and Chewing

All puppies can be very destructive during their teething period. It can be said that a Beagle puppy is part private investigator and part vacuum cleaner. The Beagle puppy is able to find things that have yet to be lost and feels everything he finds should be stored in his tummy.

"Puppy proofing" your home is a must. Your Beagle will be ingenious in getting into things he shouldn't, so you have to be far more clever and keep ahead of what your puppy might get himself into.

Provide toys that will keep the puppy busy and involved and eliminate his need for eating your needlepoint pillow or the legs off your favorite table. Just be sure to provide things that are hard to chew up. Nylabone® products such as Roar-Hide™ are ideal.

Never give your Beagle meat bones unless they are the huge beef knuckle bones. You will be amazed at how easily a Beagle can chew up and shatter most of the smaller bones. This can result in a perforated or compacted intestine.

Never give your puppy old shoes or discarded clothing to play with. Dogs can see no difference between a beat-up old sneaker you have given them and your brand new running shoes. Once you've worn shoes or clothing, they all smell *exactly* alike to your Beagle—age and cost nonwithstanding!

There is nothing a Beagle loves more than taking to the field!

Socialization:

The Beagle is by nature a happy carefree dog and takes most situations in stride. It is important, however, to accommodate the breed's natural instincts by making sure your dog is accustomed to everyday events of all kinds. Traffic, strange noises, loud or hyperactive children and strange animals can be very intimidating to a dog of any breed that has never experienced them before. Gently and gradually introduce your puppy to as many strange situations as you possibly can.

Make it a practice to take your Beagle with you everywhere whenever practical. The breed is a real crowd pleaser and you will find your dog will savor all the attention he gets.

BATHING AND GROOMING

The Beagle does not not have a long coat to contend with, but that does not mean the breed needs no grooming. Your

Beagle puppy should become accustomed to standing quietly on a grooming table for his weekly "once-over." A stiff-bristle brush will whisk away what little debris the Beagle's coat holds and a soft towel will restore the coat's shine.

Brushing should always be done in the same direction as the hair grows. You should begin at the dog's head, brushing toward the tail and down the sides and legs. This procedure will loosen the dead hair and brush it off the dog. This is the time to check the skin thoroughly for any abrasions or external parasites. Check under and inside the ears for any foul odor.

Nail Trimming

Puppyhood is a good time to accustom your Beagle to having his nails trimmed and feet inspected. The Beagle's nails are often dark and it is extremely difficult to see the blood vessel running through the center of the nail and into the "quick." The quick grows close to the end of the nail and contains very sensitive nerve endings. If the nail is allowed to grow too long, it will be impossible to cut it back to a proper length without cutting into the quick. This causes severe pain to the dog and can also result in a great deal of bleeding that can be very difficult to stop.

Roar-Hide™ is completely edible and high in protein (over 86%) and low in fat (less than one-third of 1%). Unlike common rawhide, it is safer, less messy and easier to chew.

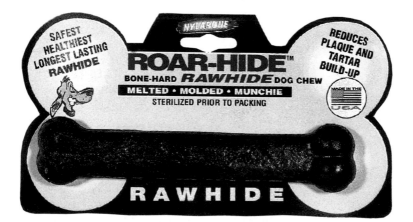

If you accustom your Beagle to grooming procedures when young, he will come to enjoy them.

The nails of a Beagle that spends most of his time indoors or on grass when outdoors can grow long very quickly. Do not allow the nails to become overgrown and then expect to cut them back easily. If your Beagle is getting plenty of exercise on cement or rough hard pavement, the nails may keep sufficiently worn down. Otherwise, the nails can grow long very quickly. They must then be carefully trimmed back with canine nail clippers, an electric nail grinder or coarse file made expressly for that purpose.

We prefer the electric nail grinder above the others because it is so easy to control and helps avoid cutting into the quick. Use of the electric grinder requires introducing your puppy to it at an early age. The instrument has a whining sound to it, very much like a dentist's drill. The noise combined with the vibration of the sanding head on the nail itself can take some getting used to, but most dogs we have used it on eventually accept it as one of life's trials. Most Beagles do not like having their nails trimmed no matter what device is used, so our own eventual decision was to use the grinder as it was less apt to damage the quick.

A bathing Beagle beauty! Only bathe your Beagle if absolutely necessary.

Should the quick accidentally be nipped in the trimming process, there are any number of blood clotting products available at pet shops that will almost immediately stem the flow of blood. It is wise to have one of these products on hand in case there is a nail trimming accident or the dog tears a nail on his own.

Always inspect your dog's feet for cracked pads. Check between the toes for splinters and thorns. Pay particular attention to any swollen or tender areas. In many sections of the country there is a weed which releases a small barbed hook-like affair that carries its seed. This hook easily finds its way into a Beagle's foot or between its toes and very quickly works its way deep into the dog's flesh. This will cause soreness and infection. These barbs should be removed by your veterinarian before serious problems result.

Bathing

If brushing is attended to regularly, bathing will seldom be necessary unless your Beagle finds his way into something that leaves his coat with a disagreeable odor. Even then, there are many products, both dry and liquid, available at your local pet store that eliminate odors and leave the coat shiny and clean. A damp wash cloth will put the Beagle that has given himself a mud bath back in shape very quickly.

Regular brushing will remove dirt from your Beagle's coat and keep it looking shiny and healthy.

HOUSEBREAKING and Training

T here is no breed of dog that cannot be trained. Some breeds appear to be slower to respond than others. Beagles are sometimes included in the "slow" category. More often than not, however, this is far more apt to be due to the trainer not being "Beagle specific" in his or her approach to the training than it is to the dog's inability to learn.

In their innate wisdom, those who created the Beagle wanted a dog that would not be dissuaded from the task of trailing game. This is all well and good except that this tenacity applies to most things the Beagle is and does. It takes effort and patience on the part of the trainer to change the Beagle's mind. Once the Beagle has learned to do something one way, it will take some effort on the part of the trainer to teach the dog a different way of doing the same thing. In other words, avoiding the bad habit in the first place is the key to training a Beagle.

The intelligent Beagle is very eager to please and easily trainable—especially when motivated!

Ease of training any dog of any breed depends in a great part upon just how much a dog depends upon his master's approval. The Beagle does want to please his owner, but he must deal with his own tenacity as well. Successfully training a Beagle depends upon your fully understanding the breed's character and dealing with it accordingly. You must always be one step ahead of your Beagle.

The key to having a well-trained Beagle is to start when he is a very young puppy with play training. While it may be difficult to remind ourselves that our wonderful Beagles trace back to the wolf, doing so will help in understanding our dogs. The wolf mother plays with her cubs and part of that play results in teaching the cubs what they may and may not do. The Beagle puppy, like his wolf cub ancestor, must think he is having fun and that he has decided on his own to do what he is participating in. Do not allow your "cute little Beagle puppy"

to do something that you would not want him to do as an adult. Give that a lot of thought and it will save you a lot of headaches later!

A puppy's biting your hands or feet, refusing to give up a toy or jumping on you or on furniture may appear cute and funny. Your allowing a puppy to do this encourages the behavior and he will continue to do this into adulthood, which will be far from cute and funny and extremely difficult to stop.

It is very important in training a Beagle that the dog is absolutely confident of his place in the "pack"— the human or humans the dog lives with. The Beagle's place in the pecking order must be below every family member and this must be clear to the dog from the first day he enters his new home.

All this is not to indicate the Beagle will avoid complying with a surly or aggressive attitude. Not at all. The Beagle is far more apt to be unconcerned or act as though he never in his life heard about the rule you are trying to enforce.

HOUSEBREAKING

Without a doubt, the best way to housebreak a Beagle is to use the "crate method." First-time dog owners are inclined to initially see using the crate method of housebreaking as cruel, but those same people will return later and thank us profusely for having suggested it in the first place. All dogs need a place of their own to retreat to and you will find the Beagle will consider his crate that place.

Use of a crate reduces housetraining time down to an absolute minimum and avoids keeping a puppy under constant stress by incessantly correcting him for making mistakes in the

This baby Beagle and his mother practice standing at attention— for a treat, of course!

house. The anti-crate advocates consider it cruel to confine a puppy for any length of time but find no problem in constantly harassing and punishing the puppy because he has wet on the carpet and relieved himself behind the sofa.

The crate used for housebreaking should only be large enough for the puppy to stand up, lie down in and stretch out comfortably. Crates are available at most pet emporiums at a wide range of prices. Ideal for Beagles are the fiberglass airline type crates in the number 200 or 300 size. These sizes will be larger than what is

Crate training is the easiest way to train your puppy because dogs do not like to soil where they eat and sleep.

Paper training is one method of housebreaking your Beagle.

needed for the very young puppy, but then it is not necessary to dash out and buy a new cage every few weeks to accommodate your Beagle's rapid spurts of growth. Simply cut a piece of plywood of a size to partition off the excess space in the very large cage and move it back as needed.

Begin using the crate to feed your puppy in. Keep the door closed and latched while the puppy is eating. When the meal is finished, open the cage and carry the puppy outdoors to the spot where you want him to learn to eliminate. As you are doing so you should consistently use the same words. Whether the words are "go out," "potty" or whatever, it makes no difference. The important point is the puppy will be learning both where to eliminate and that certain words mean something is expected.

A crate provides your dog with a safe and secure place to call his own.

In the event you do not have outdoor access or will be away from home for long periods of time, begin housebreaking by placing newspapers in some out-of-the-way corner that is easily accessible for the puppy. If you consistently take your puppy to the same spot you will reinforce the habit of going there for that purpose.

It is important that you do not let the puppy run loose after eating. Young puppies will eliminate almost immediately after eating or drinking. They will also be ready to relieve themselves when they first wake up and after playing. If you keep a watchful eye on your puppy you will quickly learn when this is about to take place. A puppy usually circles and sniffs the floor just before he will relieve himself. Do not give your puppy an opportunity to learn that he can eliminate in the house! Your house training chores will be reduced considerably if you avoid bad habits beginning in the first place.

If you are not able to watch your puppy every minute, he should be in his crate with the door securely latched. Each time you put your puppy in the crate, give him a small treat of some kind. Throw the treat to the back of the crate and encourage the puppy to walk in on his own. When he does so, praise the puppy and perhaps hand him another piece of the treat through the wires of the cage.

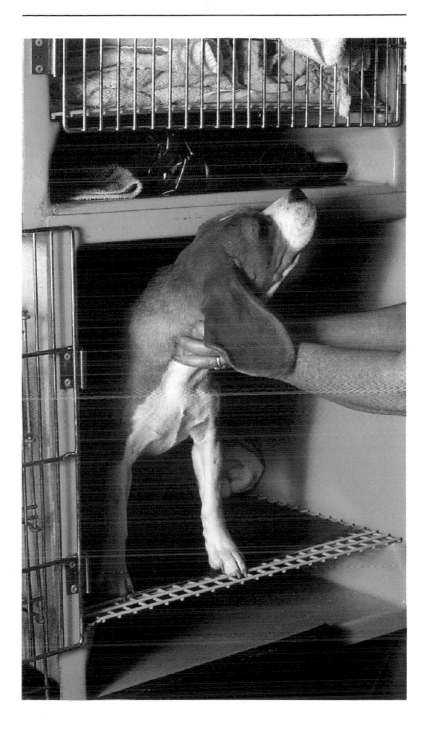

Do not succumb to your puppy's complaints about being in his crate. The puppy must learn to stay in his crate and to do so without unnecessary complaining. A quick "no" command and a tap on the crate will usually get the puppy to understand theatrics will not result in liberation.

Do understand a puppy of 8 to 12 weeks will not be able to contain himself for long periods of time. Puppies of that age must relieve themselves every few hours except at night. Your schedule must be adjusted accordingly. Also make sure your puppy has relieved both his bowels and bladder the last thing at night and do not dawdle when you wake up in the morning.

Your first priority in the morning is to get the puppy outdoors. Just how early this ritual will take place will depend much more upon your puppy than upon you. If your Beagle is like most others, there will be no doubt in your mind when he needs to be let out. You will also very quickly learn to tell the difference between the "this is an emergency" complaint and the "I just want out" grumbling. Do not test the young puppy's ability to contain himself. His vocal demand to be let out is confirmation that the housebreaking lesson is being learned.

Should you find it necessary to be away from home all day you will not be able to leave your puppy in a crate. On the other hand, do not make the mistake of allowing him to roam the house or even a large room at will. Confine the puppy to a small room or partitioned-off area and cover the floor with newspaper. Make this area large enough so that the puppy will not have to relieve himself next to his bed, food or water bowls. You will soon find the puppy will be inclined to use one particular spot to perform his bowel

and bladder functions. When you are home you must take the puppy to this exact spot to eliminate at the appropriate time.

A crate is the safest way for your dog to travel.

Basic training can lead your Beagle to bigger things! Ch. Lanbur Bridal Vale's Kellie and Ch. Lanbur Bridal Vale's Chantilly, owned by Carole Bolan, are obedience trial stars.

BASIC TRAINING

Early "puppy kindergarten," along with puppy play training, is vital if you plan to do obedience work of any kind. The AKC annually records a significant number of Beagles that have achieved Obedience titles. There are several titles that can be earned. The requirements for each can be obtained by writing the AKC and requesting their free booklet titled *Obedience Regulations*.

Where you are emotionally and the environment in which you train are just as important to your dog's training as is his state of mind at the time. Never begin training when you are irritated, distressed or preoccupied. Nor should you begin basic training in a place that interferes with you or your dog's concentration. Once the commands are understood and learned, you can begin testing your dog in public places, but at first the two of you should work in a place where you can concentrate fully upon each other.

Leash Training

It is never too early to accustom the Beagle puppy to a collar and leash. These tools are your way of keeping your dog under control. It may not be necessary for the puppy or adult Beagle to wear his collar and identification tags within the confines of your home, but no dog should ever leave home without a collar and without the leash held securely in your hand.

Begin getting your puppy accustomed to his collar by leaving it on for a few minutes at a time. Gradually extend the time you leave the collar on. Most Beagles become accustomed to their collar very quickly and forget they are even wearing one.

Once this is accomplished, attach a lightweight leash to the collar while you are playing with the puppy. Do not try to guide the puppy at first. The point here is to accustom the puppy to the feeling of having something attached to the collar.

For his safety, the come command is one of the most important things you will teach your dog. This Beagle practices with his owner.

Encourage your puppy to follow you as you move away. Should the puppy be reluctant to cooperate, coax him along with a treat of some kind. Hold the treat in front of the puppy's nose to encourage him to follow you. Just as soon as the puppy takes a few steps toward you, praise him enthusiastically and continue to do so as you continue to move along.

Make the initial sessions very brief and very enjoyable. Continue the lessons in your home or yard until the puppy is completely unconcerned about the fact that he is on a leash. With a treat in one hand and the leash in the other you can begin to use both to guide the puppy in the direction you wish to go. Your walks can begin in front of the house and eventually extend down the street and around the block. This is one lesson no puppy is too young to learn.

Every Beagle puppy deserves basic training in order to become a well-mannered pet.

The "No" Command

There is no doubt whatsoever that one of the most important commands your Beagle puppy will ever learn is the meaning of the "no" command. It is critical that the puppy learn this command just as soon as possible. One important piece of advice in using this and all other commands— *never give a command you are not prepared and able to follow through on!* The only way a puppy learns to obey commands is to realize that once issued, commands must be complied with. Learning the "no" command should start on the first day of the puppy's arrival at your home.

The "Come" Command

The next most important lesson for the Beagle puppy to learn is to come when called, therefore it is very important that the puppy learn his name as soon as possible. Constant repetition is what does the trick in teaching a puppy his name. Use the name every time you talk to your puppy.

Learning to "come" on command could save your dog's life when the two of you venture out into the world. "Come" is the command a dog must understand has to be obeyed without

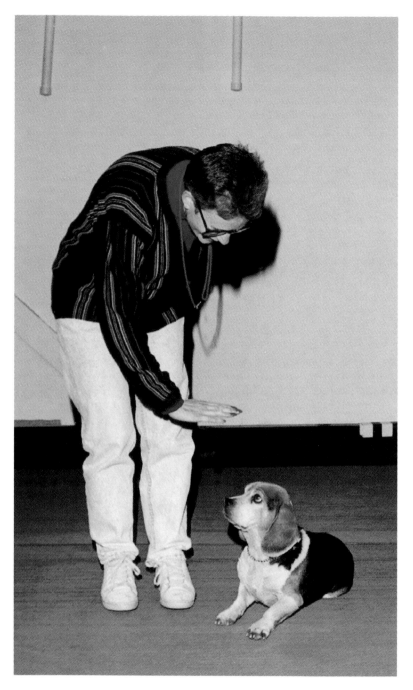

question but the dog should not associate that command with fear. Your dog's response to his name and the word "come" should always be associated with a pleasant experience such as great praise and petting or particularly in the case of the Beagle—a food treat.

Remember, in training a Beagle it is far easier to avoid the establishment of bad habits than it is to correct them once set. *Never* give the "come" command unless you are sure your Beagle puppy will come to you. The very young puppy is far more inclined to respond to learning the "come" command than the older dog. Use the command initially when the puppy is already on his way to you or give the command while walking or running away from the youngster. Clap your hands and sound very happy and excited about having the puppy join in on this "game."

The Beagle may be stubborn, but once he learns a lesson, he will remember it for the rest of his life.

The very young Beagle will normally want to stay as close to his owner as possible, especially in strange surroundings. When your puppy sees you moving away, his natural inclination will be to get close to you. This is a perfect time to use the "come" command.

Later, as the puppy grows more independent and more headstrong, as you now know a Beagle is capable of becoming, you may want to attach a long leash or rope to the puppy's collar to ensure the correct response. Do not chase or punish your puppy for not obeying the "come" command. Doing so in the initial stages of training makes the youngster associate the command with something to resist and this will result in avoidance rather than the immediate positive response you desire. It is imperative that you praise your Beagle puppy and give him a treat when he does come to you, even if he voluntarily delays responding for many minutes.

Hand signals in conjunction with verbal commands are very effective. This Beagle obeys the down command.

The "Sit" and "Stay" Commands

Just as important to your Beagle's safety (and your sanity!) as the "no" command and learning to come when called are the "sit" and "stay" commands. Even very young Beagles can learn the sit command quickly, especially if it appears to be a game and a food treat is involved.

The Beagle-in-training should always be on collar and leash for all his lessons. A Beagle is certainly not beyond getting up and walking away when he has decided something across the yard is far more interesting than your lesson!

Give the "sit" command immediately before pushing down on your Beagle's hindquarters. Praise the dog lavishly when he does sit, even though it is you who made the action take place. Again, a food treat always seems to get the lesson across to the learning Beagle.

Put your hand lightly on the dog's rear and repeat the "sit" command several times. If your dog makes an attempt to get up, repeat the command yet again while exerting pressure on the chest. Make your Beagle stay in this position for increasing lengths of time. Begin with a few seconds and increase the time as lessons progress over the following weeks.

Should your Beagle student attempt to get up or to lie down, he should be corrected by simply saying "sit" in a firm voice. This should be accompanied by returning the dog to the desired position.

Once your Beagle has begun to understand the "sit" command, you may able to get the dog to assume the position by simply putting your hand on his chest and exerting slight backward pressure.

Only when you decide your dog should get up should he be allowed to do so. Do not test the young Beagle's patience to the limits. Remember you are dealing with a baby and the attention span of any youngster is relatively short.

When you do decide the dog can get up, call his name, say "OK" and make a big fuss over him. Praise and a food treat are in order every time your Beagle responds correctly.

Once your Beagle has mastered the "sit" lesson you may start on the "stay" command. With your dog on leash and facing you, command him to "sit," then take a step or two back. If your dog attempts to get up to follow firmly say, "Sit, stay!" While you are saying this raise your hand, palm toward the dog, and again command "stay!"

Any attempt on your dog's part to get up must be corrected at once, returning him to the sit position and repeating "stay!"

Once your dog begins to understand what you want, you can gradually increase the distance you step back. With a long leash attached to your dog's collar (even a clothesline will do) start with a few steps and gradually increase the distance to several yards. Your Beagle must eventually learn the "sit, stay" command must be obeyed no matter how far away you are.

The Beagle can provide his owner with many pleasant hours of outdoor activity in the field. Branko's Beagles Telli-Prop is pictured here winning a field trial championship.

Later on, with advanced training, your dog will learn the command is to be obeyed even when you move entirely out of sight.

Avoid calling the dog *to you* at first. This makes the dog overly anxious to get up and come to you. Until your Beagle masters the "sit" lesson and is able to remain in the sit position for as long as you dictate, walk back to your dog and say "OK," a signal that the command is over. Later, when your dog becomes more reliable in this respect, you can call him to you.

The "sit, stay" lesson can take considerable time and patience especially with the Beagle puppy whose attention span will be very short. It is best to keep the "stay" part of the lesson to a minimum until a Beagle is at least five or six months old. Everything in a very young Beagle's makeup will urge him to follow you wherever you go. Forcing a very young puppy to operate against his natural instincts can be bewildering for him.

The "Down" Command

Once your Beagle has mastered the "sit" and "stay" commands, you may begin work on "down." This is the single word command for lie down. Use the "down" command *only* when you want the dog to lie down. If you want your Beagle to get off your sofa or to stop jumping up on people, use the "off" command. Do not interchange these two commands. Doing so will only serve to confuse your dog and evoking the right response will become next to impossible.

The "down" position is especially useful if you want your Beagle to remain in a particular place for a long period of time. A Beagle is far more inclined to stay put when he is lying down than when he is sitting. However, lying in the "correct" position may not be as appealing to your Beagle as perhaps stretching out on his side or even on his back! Correct obedience performance dictates that your dog lie on his stomach with his front legs stretched out ahead.

Teaching your Beagle to obey this command properly may take more time and patience than the previous lessons the two of you have undertaken. It is believed by some animal behaviorists that assuming the "down" position somehow represents submissiveness to the dog. In the end, once the "down" command has become a part of your Beagle's repertory, it seems to be more relaxing for the dog and you will find he seems less inclined to get up and wander off.

With your Beagle sitting in front of and facing you, hold a treat in your right hand with the excess part of the leash in your left hand. Hold the treat under the dog's nose and slowly bring your hand down to the ground. Your dog will follow the treat with his head and neck. As he does, give the command "down."

An alternative method of getting your Beagle headed into the down position is to move around to the dog's right side and as you draw his attention downward with your right hand, slide your left arm under the dog's front legs and gently slide them forward. In the case of the smaller Beagle or puppy you will undoubtedly have to be on your knees next to the youngster.

Janet Graham's ten-week-old puppy is happy to be a centerfold model.

As your Beagle's forelegs begin to slide out to his front, keep moving the treat along the ground until the dog's whole body is lying on the ground while you continually repeat "down." Once your dog has assumed the position you desire, give him the treat and a lot of praise. Continue assisting your Beagle into the "down" position until he does so on his own. Be firm and be patient.

Be sure to securely fasten your Beagle's collar. "Choke collars" must be put on the dog properly.

The "Heel" Command

In learning to heel, your Beagle will walk on your left side with his shoulder next to your leg no matter which direction you might go or how quickly you turn. Teaching your Beagle to heel will not only make your daily walks far more enjoyable, it will make a far more tractable companion when the two of you are in crowded or confusing situations. An untrained Beagle, even when on a leash, can be a nuisance to control, particularly if you are carrying packages, opening doors or manipulating stairs or elevators. Beagles want to be with you where ever you go, so training him to walk along in the correct position is usually not much of a problem.

We have found a link-chain training collar is very useful for the heeling lesson. It provides both quick pressure around the neck and a snapping sound, both of which get the dog's attention. Erroneously referred to as a "choke collar," the link-chain collar used properly will not choke the dog. The pet shop at which you purchase the training collar will be able to show you the proper way to put this collar on your dog.

In the beginning, when you are training your Beagle puppy to walk along on the leash, you should accustom the youngster to walk on your left side. The leash should cross your body from the dog's collar to your right hand. The excess portion of the leash will be folded into your right hand and your left hand on the leash will be used to make corrections with the leash.

A quick, short jerk on the leash with your left hand will keep your Beagle from lunging from side to side, pulling ahead or lagging back. As you make a correction, give the "heel" command. Always keep the leash slack as long as your dog maintains the proper position at your side.

If your dog begins to drift away, give the leash a sharp jerk and guide the dog back to the correct position and give the "heel" command. *Do not pull on the lead with steady pressure!* What is needed is a sharp but gentle jerking motion to get your dog's attention. Remember, it is always *"jerk and release."*

TRAINING CLASSES

There are actually few limits to what a patient, consistent Beagle owner (and the accent is most definitely on *patient* and *consistent!*) can teach his or her dog. A lot of praise (and food treats!) will make the road to success much easier for the both of you.

For advanced obedience work beyond the basics, it is wise for the Beagle owner to consider local professional assistance. Professional trainers have had long standing experience in avoiding the pitfalls of obedience training and can help you to avoid them as well. This training assistance can be obtained in many ways. The strange dogs and new people encountered at training classes are particularly good for your Beagle's socialization. There are free-of-charge classes at many parks and recreation facilities, as well as very formal and sometimes very expensive individual lessons with private trainers.

There are also some obedience schools that will take your Beagle and train him for you. However, unless your schedule provides no time at all to train your own dog, having someone else train the

These two puppies practice sitting still—for puppies, that's the hardest part!

A versatile hunting dog, the Beagle excels in many events. This Beagle works a rabbit track at a field trial. dog for you would be last on our list of recommendations. The rapport that develops between the owner who has trained his or her Beagle to be a pleasant companion and good canine citizen is very special— well worth the time and patience it requires to achieve.

BEAGLE VERSATILITY
Once your Beagle has been taught his basic manners, there are countless ways that the two of you can participate in enjoyable events. The breed is highly successful in conformation shows and has proven he can also do well in obedience competition. Certainly there is nothing he will enjoy more than field work. Field work can take the form of formal field trials or the actual hunt.

Field Trials
Although we seldom require a Beagle to chase a bunny out of the woods to help bring home food for the table, there is a thrill to be had in hearing the sound of the Beagle baying on the trail. Today organized Beagle field trials are divided into

two categories: cottontail trials and hare trials. Cottontail trials are those in which the Beagles run in pairs or very small packs and are run without limit. Hare trials are always run in packs, usually large packs.

There are both "fun" and "licensed" trials. There are exacting rules for the licensed events and field trial championships can be obtained by successful competitors. Information regarding the rules governing these licensed events can be obtained from the AKC. The fun trials are held by local organizations and are mounted purely for the enjoyment of those participating.

When it comes to tracking, there are few better than the Beagle. U-CD Harris, CD, TDX, owned by Les Brandt, uses his nose to his advantage.

Hunting

When it comes to rabbit hunting, there is no better dog than the Beagle. Those who use the Beagle for hunting small game find the breed has few equals.

Canine Good Citizen

Less demanding but certainly a good introduction to more advanced obedience training are the requirements for a Canine Good Citizen certificate. These certificates are earned by a dog passing a ten-part test as designed by the American Kennel Club. These tests include cleanliness and grooming, socialization, obeying simple commands and general tractability. As the name implies, any dog capable of earning the certificate can only be a better friend and companion.

Therapy Dogs

Beagles can perform an extremely valuable service by visiting homes for the aged, orphanages and hospitals. Beagles love people and people of all ages are easily seduced by a Beagle's sweet expression and gentle ways. It is amazing to see how kind and gentle Beagles are with small children and with people who are ill or feeble. It has been proven these visits provide great therapeutic value to the patients.

The well trained Beagle can provide a whole world of activities for the owner. You are only limited by the amount of time you wish to invest in this remarkable breed.

SPORT of Purebred Dogs

Welcome to the exciting and sometimes frustrating sport of dogs. No doubt you are trying to learn more about dogs or you wouldn't be deep into this book. This section covers the basics that may entice you, further your knowledge and help you to understand the dog world.

Dog showing has been a very popular sport for a long time and has been taken quite seriously by some. Others only enjoy it as a hobby.

U-CD Gabriel'S Chelsea Morning, CDX, TDX, Can. CD, CGC, TDI, owned by Denise Nord winning High in Trial.

The Kennel Club in England was formed in 1859, the American Kennel Club was established in 1884 and the Canadian Kennel Club was formed in 1888. The purpose of these clubs was to register purebred dogs and maintain their Stud Books. In the beginning, the concept of registering dogs was not readily accepted. More than 36 million dogs have been enrolled in the AKC Stud Book since its inception in 1888. Presently the kennel clubs not only register dogs but adopt and enforce rules and regulations governing dog shows, obedience trials and field trials. Over the years they have fostered and encouraged interest in the health and welfare of the purebred dog. They routinely donate funds to veterinary research for study on genetic disorders.

Successful showing requires dedication and hard work, but most of all, it should be an enjoyable experience for both the handlers and the dogs.

Below are the addresses of the kennel clubs in the United States, Great Britain and Canada.

The American Kennel Club
51 Madison Avenue
New York, NY 10010
(Their registry is located at: 5580 Centerview Drive, STE 200, Raleigh, NC 27606-3390)

The Kennel Club
1 Clarges Street
Piccadilly, London, WIY 8AB, England

The Canadian Kennel Club
111 Eglinton Avenue
East Toronto, Ontario M6S 4V7
Canada

According to the standard, Beagles may be any true hound color. This is a well-marked red and white female.

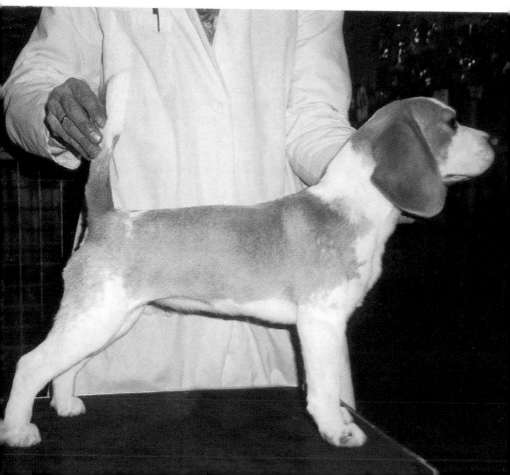

U-CD, Gabriel's Chelsea Morning, CDX, TDX, Can. CD, CGC, TDI, owned by Denise Nord shines on the agility course.

Today there are numerous activities that are enjoyable for both the dog and the handler. Some of the activities include conformation showing, obedience competition, tracking, agility, the Canine Good Citizen Certificate, and a wide range of instinct tests that vary from breed to breed. Where you start depends upon your goals which early on may not be readily apparent.

Puppy Kindergarten

Every puppy will benefit from this class. PKT is the foundation for all future dog activities from conformation to "couch potatoes." Pet owners should make an effort to attend even if they never expect to show their dog. The class is designed for puppies about three months of age with graduation at approximately five months of age. All the puppies will be in the same age group and, even though some may be a little unruly, there should not be any real problem. This class will teach the puppy some beginning obedience. As in all obedience classes the owner learns how to train his own dog. The PKT class gives the puppy the opportunity to interact with other puppies in the same age group and exposes him to strangers, which is very important. Some dogs grow up with behavior problems, one of them being fear of strangers. As you can see, there can be much to gain from this class.

There are some basic obedience exercises that every dog should learn. Some of these can be started with puppy kindergarten.

CONFORMATION

Conformation showing is our oldest dog show sport. This type of showing is based on the dog's appearance—that is his structure, movement and attitude. When considering this type of showing, you need to be aware of your breed's standard and be able to evaluate your dog compared to that standard. The breeder of your puppy or other experienced breeders would be good sources for such an evaluation. Puppies can go through lots of changes over a period of time. Many puppies start out as promising hopefuls and then after maturing may be disappointing as show candidates. Even so this should not deter them from being excellent pets.

Usually conformation training classes are offered by the local kennel or obedience clubs. These are excellent places for training puppies. The puppy should be able to walk on a lead before entering such a class. Proper ring procedure and technique for posing (stacking) the dog will be demonstrated as well as gaiting the dog. Usually certain patterns are used in the ring such as the triangle or the "L." Conformation class, like the PKT class, will give your youngster the opportunity to socialize with different breeds of dogs and humans too.

It takes some time to learn the routine of conformation showing. Usually one starts at the puppy matches that may be AKC Sanctioned or Fun Matches. These matches are generally for puppies from two or three months to a year old, and there may be classes for the adult over the age of 12 months. Similar to point shows, the classes are divided by sex and after completion of the classes in that breed or variety, the class winners compete for Best of Breed or Variety. The winner goes on to compete in the Group and the Group winners compete for Best in Match. No championship points are awarded for match wins.

A few matches can be great training for puppies even though there is no intention to go on showing. Matches enable the puppy to meet new people and be handled by a stranger—the judge. It is also a change of environment, which broadens the horizon for both dog and handler. Matches and other dog activities boost the confidence of the handler and especially the younger handlers.

Earning an AKC championship is built on a point system, which is different from Great Britain. To become an AKC Champion of Record the dog must earn 15 points. The number of points earned each time depends upon the number of dogs in competition. The number of points available at each show depends upon the breed, its sex and the location of the show.

Trick or treat! Beagles enjoy having fun as much as their owners.

The United States is divided into ten AKC zones. Each zone has its own set of points. The purpose of the zones is to try to equalize the points available from breed to breed and area to area. The AKC adjusts the point scale annually.

The number of points that can be won at a show are between one and five. Three-, four- and five-point wins are considered majors. Not only does the dog need 15 points won under three different judges, but those points must include two majors under two different judges. Canada also works on a point system but majors are not required.

Dogs always show before bitches. The classes available to those seeking points are: Puppy (which may be divided into 6 to 9 months and 9 to 12 months); 12 to 18 months; Novice; Bred-by-Exhibitor; American-bred; and Open. The class winners of the same sex of each breed or variety compete against each other for Winners Dog and Winners Bitch. A Reserve Winners Dog and Reserve Winners Bitch are also awarded but do not carry any points unless the Winners win is disallowed by AKC. The Winners Dog and Bitch compete with the specials (those dogs that have attained championship) for Best of Breed or Variety,

All Beagle puppies can benefit from early training to teach them basic obedience and good manners.

Best of Winners and Best of Opposite Sex. It is possible to pick up an extra point or even a major if the points are higher for the defeated winner than those of Best of Winners. The latter would get the higher total from the defeated winner.

At an all-breed show, each Best of Breed or Variety winner will go on to his respective Group and then the Group winners will compete against each other for Best in Show. There are seven Groups: Sporting, Hounds, Working, Terriers, Toys, Non-Sporting and Herding. Obviously there are no Groups at speciality shows (those shows that have only one breed or a show such as the American Spaniel Club's Flushing Spaniel Show, which is for all flushing spaniel breeds).

Earning a championship in England is somewhat different since they do not have a point system. Challenge Certificates are awarded if the judge feels the dog is deserving regardless of the number of dogs in competition. A dog must earn three

A talented Beagle participates in an obedience trail.

Challenge Certificates under three different judges, with at least one of these Certificates being won after the age of 12 months. Competition is very strong and entries may be higher than they are in the U.S. The Kennel Club's Challenge Certificates are only available at Championship Shows.

In England, The Kennel Club regulations require that certain dogs, Border Collies and Gundog breeds, qualify in a working capacity (i.e., obedience or field trials) before becoming a full Champion. If they do not qualify in the working aspect, then they are designated a Show Champion, which is equivalent to the AKC's Champion of Record. A Gundog may be granted the title of Field Trial Champion (FT Ch.) if it passes all the tests in the field but would also have to qualify in conformation before becoming a full Champion. A Border Collie that earns the title of Obedience Champion (Ob Ch.) must also qualify in the conformation ring before becoming a Champion.

The U.S. doesn't have a designation full Champion but does award for Dual and Triple Champions. The Dual Champion must be a Champion of Record, and either Champion Tracker, Herding Champion, Obedience Trial Champion or Field Champion. Any dog that has been awarded the titles of Champion of Record, and any two of the following: Champion Tracker, Herding Champion, Obedience Trial Champion or Field Champion, may be designated as a Triple Champion.

The shows in England seem to put more emphasis on breeder judges than those in the U.S. There is much competition within the breeds. Therefore the quality of the individual breeds should be very good. In the United States we tend to have more "all around judges" (those that judge multiple breeds) and use the breeder judges at the specialty shows. Breeder judges are more familiar with their own breed since they are actively breeding that breed or did so at one time. Americans emphasize Group and Best in Show wins and promote them accordingly.

The shows in England can be very large and extend over several days, with the Groups being scheduled on different days. Though multi-day shows are not common in the U.S., there are cluster shows, where several different clubs will use the same show site over consecutive days.

Westminster Kennel Club is our most prestigious show although the entry is limited to 2500. In recent years, entry has been limited to Champions. This show is more formal than the majority of the shows with the judges wearing formal attire and the handlers fashionably dressed. In most instances the quality of the dogs is superb. After all, it is a show of Champions. It is a good show to study the AKC registered breeds and is by far the most exciting—especially since it is televised! WKC is one of the few shows in this country that is still benched. This means the dog must be in his benched area during the show hours except when he is being groomed, in the ring, or being exercised.

Typically, the handlers are very particular about their appearances. They are careful not to wear something that will detract from their dog but will perhaps enhance it. American ring procedure is quite formal compared to that of other countries. There is a certain etiquette expected between the judge and exhibitor and among the other exhibitors. Of course it is not always the case but the judge is supposed to be polite, not engaging in small talk or acknowledging how well he knows the handler. There is a more informal and relaxed atmosphere at the shows in other countries. For instance, the dress code is more casual. I can see where this might be more fun for the exhibitor and especially for the novice. The U.S. is very handler-oriented in many of the breeds. It is true, in most instances, that the experienced professional handler can present the dog better and will have a feel for what a judge likes.

In England, Crufts is The Kennel Club's own show and is most assuredly the largest dog show in the world. They've been known to have an entry of nearly 20,000, and the show lasts four days. Entry is only gained by qualifying through winning in specified classes at another Championship Show. Westminster is strictly conformation, but Crufts exhibitors and spectators enjoy not only conformation but obedience, agility and a multitude of exhibitions as well. Obedience was admitted in 1957 and agility in 1983.

Preparing for a future in the ring, show puppies learn to "stack" at an early age.

If you are handling your own dog, please give some consideration to your apparel. For sure the dress code at matches is more informal than the point shows. However, you should wear something a little more appropriate than beach attire or ragged jeans and bare feet. If you check out the handlers and see what is presently fashionable, you'll catch on. Men usually dress with a shirt and tie and a nice sports coat. Whether you are male or female, you will want to wear comfortable clothes and shoes. You need to be able to run with your dog and you certainly don't want to take a chance of

Handlers gait their dogs around the ring so judges can evaluate their movement and body structure.

falling and hurting yourself. Heaven forbid, if nothing else, you'll upset your dog. Women usually wear a dress or two-piece outfit, preferably with pockets to carry bait, comb, brush, etc. In this case men are the lucky ones with all their pockets. Ladies, think about where your dress will be if you need to kneel on the floor and also think about running. Does it allow freedom to do so?

You need to take along dog; crate; ex pen (if you use one); extra newspaper; water pail and water; all required grooming equipment, including hair dryer and extension cord; table; chair for you; bait for dog and lunch for you and friends; and, last but not least, clean up materials, such as plastic bags, paper towels, and perhaps a bath towel and some shampoo— just in case. Don't forget your entry confirmation and directions to the show.

If you are showing in obedience, then you will want to wear pants. Many of our top obedience handlers wear pants that are color-coordinated with their dogs. The philosophy is that imperfections in the black dog will be less obvious next to your black pants.

Beagles can do anything! This is the 1995 Drill Team at the National Beagle Club National Specialty Show.

Whether you are showing in conformation, Junior Showmanship or obedience, you need to watch the clock and be sure you are not late. It is customary to pick up your conformation armband a few minutes before the start of the class. They will not wait for you and if you are on the show grounds and not in the ring, you will upset everyone. It's a little more complicated picking up your obedience armband if you show later in the class. If you have not picked up your armband and they get to your number, you may not be allowed to show. It's best to pick up your armband early, but then you may show earlier than expected if other handlers don't pick up. Customarily all conflicts should be discussed with the judge prior to the start of the class.

Junior Showmanship

The Junior Showmanship Class is a wonderful way to build self confidence even if there are no aspirations of staying with the dog-show game later in life. Frequently, Junior Showmanship becomes the background of those who become successful exhibitors/handlers in the future. In some instances it is taken very seriously, and success is measured in terms of wins. The Junior Handler is judged solely on his ability and skill in presenting his dog. The dog's conformation is not to be considered by the judge. Even so the condition and grooming of the dog may be a reflection upon the handler.

Usually the matches and point shows include different classes. The Junior Handler's dog may be entered in a breed or

obedience class and even shown by another person in that class. Junior Showmanship classes are usually divided by age and perhaps sex. The age is determined by the handler's age on the day of the show.

CANINE GOOD CITIZEN

The AKC sponsors a program to encourage dog owners to train their dogs. Local clubs perform the pass/fail tests, and dogs who pass are awarded a Canine Good Citizen Certificate. Proof of vaccination is required at the time of participation. The test includes:

1. Accepting a friendly stranger.
2. Sitting politely for petting.
3. Appearance and grooming.
4. Walking on a loose leash.
5. Walking through a crowd.
6. Sit and down on command/ staying in place.
7. Come when called.
8. Reaction to another dog.
9. Reactions to distractions.
10. Supervised separation.

In order to become a Canine Good Citizen, your Beagle must be able to accept handling and petting.

If more effort was made by pet owners to accomplish these exercises, fewer dogs would be cast off to the humane shelter.

OBEDIENCE

Obedience is necessary, without a doubt, but it can also become a wonderful hobby or even an obsession. Obedience classes and competition can provide wonderful companionship, not only with your dog but with your classmates or fellow competitors. It is always gratifying to discuss your dog's problems with others who have had similar experiences. The AKC acknowledged Obedience around 1936, and it has changed tremendously even though many of the exercises are basically the same. Today, obedience competition is

Training for dog shows or any type of competition allows the dog and owner to develop a closeness through working together.

just that—very competitive. Even so, it is possible for every obedience exhibitor to come home a winner (by earning qualifying scores) even though he/she may not earn a placement in the class.

Hermann J. Mueller's sextet of Beagle champions are perfect examples of the breed's legendary sociability.

Most of the obedience titles are awarded after earning three qualifying scores (legs) in the appropriate class under three different judges. These classes offer a perfect score of 200, which is extremely rare. Each of the class exercises has its own point value. A leg is earned after receiving a score of at least 170 and at least 50 percent of the points available in each exercise. The titles are:

Companion Dog—CD

This is called the Novice Class and the exercises are:

1. Heel on leash and figure 8	40 points
2. Stand for examination	30 points
3. Heel free	40 points
4. Recall	30 points
5. Long sit—one minute	30 points
6. Long down—three minutes	30 points
Maximum total score	200 points

Companion Dog Excellent—CDX

This is the Open Class and the exercises are:

1. Heel off leash and figure 8	40 points
2. Drop on recall	30 points
3. Retrieve on flat	20 points
4. Retrieve over high jump	30 points
5. Broad jump	20 points
6. Long sit—three minutes (out of sight)	30 points
7. Long down—five minutes (out of sight)	30 points
Maximum total score	200 points

Utility Dog—UD

The Utility Class exercises are:

1. Signal Exercise	40 points
2. Scent discrimination-Article 1	30 points
3. Scent discrimination-Article 2	30 points
4. Directed retrieve	30 points
5. Moving stand and examination	30 points
6. Directed jumping	40 points
Maximum total score	200 points

After achieving the UD title, you may feel inclined to go after the UDX and/or OTCh. The UDX (Utility Dog Excellent) title went into effect in January 1994. It is not easily attained. The title requires qualifying simultaneously ten times in Open B and Utility B but not necessarily at consecutive shows.

The OTCh (Obedience Trial Champion) is awarded after the dog has earned his UD and then goes on to earn 100 championship points, a first place in Utility, a first place in Open and another first place in either class. The placements must be won under three different judges at all-breed obedience trials. The points are determined by the number of

As a field dog, the Beagle is a sharp and efficeint tracker, possessing endless energy and endurance.

dogs competing in the Open B and Utility B classes. The OTCh title precedes the dog's name.

Obedience matches (AKC Sanctioned, Fun, and Show and Go) are usually available. Usually they are sponsored by the local obedience clubs. When preparing an obedience dog for a title, you will find matches very helpful. Fun Matches and Show and Go Matches are more lenient in allowing you to make corrections in the ring. This type of training is usually very necessary for the Open and Utility Classes. AKC Sanctioned Obedience Matches do not allow corrections in the ring since they must abide by the AKC Obedience Regulations. If you are interested in showing in obedience, then you should contact the AKC for a copy of the Obedience Regulations.

Tracking

Tracking is officially classified obedience. There are three tracking titles available: Tracking Dog (TD), Tracking Dog Excellent (TDX), Variable Surface Tracking (VST). If all three tracking titles are obtained, then the dog officially becomes a CT (Champion Tracker). The CT will go in front of the dog's name.

A TD may be earned anytime and does not have to follow the other obedience titles. There are many exhibitors that prefer tracking to obedience, and there are others who do both.

Tracking Dog—TD

A dog must be certified by an AKC tracking judge that he is ready to perform in an AKC test. The AKC can provide the names of tracking judges in your area that you can contact for certification. Depending on where you live, you may have to travel a distance if there is no local tracking judge. The certification track will be equivalent to a regular AKC track. A regulation track must be 440 to 500 yards long with at least two right-angle turns out in the open. The track will be aged 30 minutes to two hours. The handler has two starting flags at the beginning of the track to indicate the direction started. The dog works on a harness and 40-foot lead and must work at least 20 feet in front of the handler. An article (either a dark glove or wallet) will be dropped at the end of the track, and the dog must indicate it but not necessarily retrieve it.

People always ask what the dog tracks. Initially, the beginner on the short-aged track tracks the tracklayer. Eventually the dog learns to track the disturbed vegetation and learns to differentiate between tracks. Getting started with tracking requires reading the AKC regulations and a good book on tracking plus finding other tracking enthusiasts. Work on the buddy system. That is—lay tracks for each other so you can practice blind tracks. It is possible to train on your own, but if you are a beginner, it is a lot more entertaining to track with a buddy. It's rewarding seeing the dog use his natural ability.

Tracking Dog Excellent—TDX

The TDX track is 800 to 1000 yards long and is aged three to five hours. There will be five to seven turns. An article is left at the starting flag, and three other articles must be indicated on the track. There is only one flag at the start, so it is a blind start. Approximately one and a half hours after the track is laid, two

"We're hunting wabbits!" Tracking is one aspect of obedience that Beagles have a natural talent and affinity.

tracklayers will cross over the track at two different places to test the dog's ability to stay with the original track. There will be at least two obstacles on the track such as a change of cover, fences, creeks, ditches, etc. The dog must have a TD before entering a TDX. There is no certification required for a TDX.

Variable Surface Tracking–VST

This test came into effect September 1995. The dog must have a TD earned at least six months prior to entering this test. The track is 600 to 800 yards long and shall have a minimum of three different surfaces. Vegetation shall be included along with two areas devoid of vegetation such as concrete, asphalt, gravel, sand, hard pan or mulch. The areas devoid of vegetation shall comprise at least one-third to one-half of the track. The track is aged three to five hours. There will be four to eight turns and four numbered articles including one leather, one plastic, one metal and one fabric dropped on the track. There is one starting flag. The handler will work at least 10 feet from the dog.

Obedience trial star Chelsea takes the agility course obstacle in stride.

Agility is an action-packed sport that thrills both participants and spectators. Squiggles, owned by Marietta Huber, maneuvers the weave poles.

AGILITY

Agility was first introduced by John Varlcy in England at the Crufts Dog Show, February 1978, but Peter Meanwell, competitor and judge, actually developed the idea. It was officially recognized in the early '80s. Agility is extremely popular in England and Canada and growing in popularity in the U.S. The AKC acknowledged agility in August 1994. Dogs must be at least 12 months of age to be entered. It is a fascinating sport that the dog, handler and spectators enjoy to the utmost. Agility is a spectator sport! The dog performs off lead. The handler either runs with his dog or positions himself on the course and directs his dog with verbal and hand signals over a timed course over or through a variety of obstacles including a time out or pause. One of the main drawbacks to agility is finding a place to train. The obstacles take up a lot of space and it is very time consuming to put up and take down courses.

As called for by the breed standard, the Beagle's legs are straight with plenty of bone and possessing strength and substance.

The titles earned at AKC agility trials are Novice Agility Dog (NAD), Open Agility Dog (OAD), Agility Dog Excellent (ADX), and Master Agility Excellent (MAX). In order to acquire an agility title, a dog must earn a qualifying score in its respective class on three separate occasions under two different judges. The MAX will be awarded after earning ten qualifying scores in the Agility Excellent Class.

PERFORMANCE TESTS

During the last decade the American Kennel Club has promoted performance tests—those events that test the different breeds' natural abilities. This type of event encourages a handler to devote even more time to his dog and retain the natural instincts of his breed heritage. It is an important part of the wonderful world of dogs.

GENERAL INFORMATION

Obedience, tracking and agility allow the purebred dog with an Indefinite Listing Privilege (ILP) number or a limited registration to be exhibited and earn titles. Application must be made to the AKC for an ILP number.

The American Kennel Club publishes a monthly *Events* magazine that is part of the *Gazette*, their official journal for the sport of purebred dogs. The *Events* section lists upcoming shows and the secretary or superintendent for them. The majority of the conformation shows in the U.S. are overseen by licensed superintendents. Generally the entry closing date is approximately two-and-a-half weeks before the actual show. Point shows are fairly expensive, while the match shows cost about one third of the point show entry fee. Match shows usually take entries the day of the show but some are pre-entry.

Beagles love to use their noses and there are many organized activities, such as field trials and tracking events, in which this talent can be put to good use.

The best way to find match show information is through your local kennel club. Upon asking, the AKC can provide you with a list of superintendents, and you can write and ask to be put on their mailing lists.

Obedience trial and tracking test information is available through the AKC. Frequently these events are not superintended, but put on by the host club. Therefore you would make the entry with the event's secretary.

As you have read, there are numerous activities you can share with your dog. Regardless what you do, it does take teamwork. Your dog can only benefit from your attention and training. We hope this chapter has enlightened you and hope, if nothing else, you will attend a show here and there. Perhaps you will start with a puppy kindergarten class, and who knows where it may lead!

HEALTH CARE

Veterinary medicine has become far more sophisticated than what was available to our ancestors. This can be attributed to the increase in household pets and consequently the demand for better care for them. Also human medicine has become far more complex. Today diagnostic testing in veterinary medicine parallels human diagnostics. Because of better technology we can expect our pets to live healthier lives thereby increasing their life spans.

THE FIRST CHECK UP

You will want to take your new puppy/dog in for its first check up within 48 to 72 hours after acquiring it. Many breeders strongly recommend this check up and so do the humane shelters. A puppy/dog can appear healthy but it may have a serious problem that is not apparent to the layman. Most pets have some type of a minor flaw that may never cause a real problem.

Unfortunately if he/she should have a serious problem, you will want to consider the consequences of keeping the pet and the attachments that will be formed, which may be broken prematurely. Keep in mind there are many healthy dogs looking for good homes.

Take your new Beagle puppy to the veterinarian within 48 hours of taking him home.

This first check up is a good time to establish yourself with the veterinarian and learn the office policy regarding their hours and how they handle emergencies. Usually the breeder or another conscientious pet owner is a good reference for locating a capable veterinarian. You should be aware that not all veterinarians give the same quality of service.

Your vulnerable little puppy will depend on you to provide him with the health care he requires.

Maternal antibodies protect puppies from disease the first few weeks of life. Vaccinations are needed because these antibodies are only temporarily effective.

Please do not make your selection on the least expensive clinic, as they may be short changing your pet. There is the possibility that eventually it will cost you

more due to improper diagnosis, treatment, etc. If you are selecting a new veterinarian, feel free to ask for a tour of the clinic. You should inquire about making an appointment for a tour since all clinics are working clinics, and therefore may not be available all day for sightseers. You may worry less if you see where your pet will be spending the day if he ever needs to be hospitalized.

Proper health care and maintenance are important to your Beagle's quality of life.

THE PHYSICAL EXAM

Your veterinarian will check your pet's overall condition, which includes listening to the heart; checking the respiration; feeling the abdomen, muscles and joints; checking the mouth, which includes the gum color and signs of gum disease along with plaque buildup; checking the ears for signs of an infection or ear mites; examining the eyes; and, last but not least, checking the condition of the skin and coat.

He should ask you questions regarding your pet's eating and elimination habits and invite you to relay your questions. It is a good idea to prepare a list so as not to forget anything. He should discuss the proper diet and the quantity to be fed. If this should differ from your breeder's recommendation, then you should convey to him the breeder's choice and see if he approves. If he recommends changing the diet, then this should be done over a few days so as not to cause a gastrointestinal upset. It is customary to take in a fresh stool sample (just a small amount) for a test for intestinal parasites. It must be fresh, preferably within 12 hours, since the eggs hatch quickly and after hatching will not be observed under the microscope. If your pet isn't obliging then, usually the technician can take one in the clinic.

Find out what vaccinations your puppy has received and when his next one is scheduled before taking him home.

Immunizations

It is important that you take your puppy/dog's vaccination record with you on your first visit. In case of a puppy, presumably the breeder has seen to the vaccinations up to the time you acquired custody. Veterinarians differ in their vaccination protocol. It is not unusual for your puppy to have received vaccinations for distemper, hepatitis, leptospirosis, parvovirus and parainfluenza every two to three weeks from the age of five or six weeks. Usually this is a combined injection and is typically called the DHLPP. The DHLPP is given through at least 12 to 14 weeks of age, and it is customary to continue with another parvovirus vaccine at 16 to 18 weeks. You may wonder why so many immunizations are necessary. No one knows for sure when the puppy's maternal antibodies are gone, although it is customarily accepted that distemper antibodies are gone by 12 weeks. Usually parvovirus antibodies are gone by 16 to 18 weeks of age. However, it is possible for the maternal antibodies to be gone at a much earlier age or even a later age. Therefore immunizations are started at an early age. The vaccine will not give immunity as long as there are maternal antibodies.

The rabies vaccination is given at three or six months of age depending on your local laws. A vaccine for bordetella (kennel cough) is advisable and can be given anytime from the age of five weeks. The coronavirus is not commonly given unless there is a problem locally. The Lyme vaccine is necessary in endemic areas. Lyme disease has been reported in 47 states.

Distemper

This is virtually an incurable disease. If the dog recovers, he is subject to severe nervous disorders. The virus attacks every tissue in the body and resembles a bad cold with a fever. It can cause a runny nose and eyes and cause gastrointestinal disorders, including a poor appetite, vomiting and diarrhea. The virus is carried by raccoons, foxes, wolves, mink and other dogs. Unvaccinated youngsters and senior citizens are very susceptible. This is still a common disease.

Hepatitis

This is a virus that is most serious in very young dogs. It is spread by contact with an infected animal or its stool or urine.

The virus affects the liver and kidneys and is characterized by high fever, depression and lack of appetite. Recovered animals may be afflicted with chronic illnesses.

Leptospirosis

This is a bacterial disease transmitted by contact with the urine of an infected dog, rat or other wildlife. It produces severe symptoms of fever, depression, jaundice and internal bleeding and was fatal before the vaccine was developed. Recovered dogs can be carriers, and the disease can be transmitted from dogs to humans.

Parvovirus

This was first noted in the late 1970s and is still a fatal disease. However, with proper vaccinations, early diagnosis and prompt treatment, it is a manageable disease. It attacks the bone marrow and intestinal tract. The symptoms include depression, loss of appetite,

Your Beagle will require booster shots every year to keep his immunizations up to date.

vomiting, diarrhea and collapse. Immediate medical attention is of the essence.

Rabies

This is shed in the saliva and is carried by raccoons, skunks, foxes, other dogs and cats. It attacks nerve tissue, resulting in paralysis and death. Rabies can be transmitted to people and is virtually always fatal. This disease is reappearing in the suburbs.

Bordetella (Kennel Cough)

The symptoms are coughing, sneezing, hacking and retching accompanied by nasal discharge usually lasting from a few days to several weeks. There are several disease-producing organisms responsible for this disease. The present vaccines are helpful but do not protect for all the strains. It usually is not life threatening but in some instances it can progress to a serious bronchopneumonia. The disease is highly contagious. The vaccination should be given routinely for dogs that come in contact with other dogs, such as through boarding, training class or visits to the groomer.

Bordetella attached to canine cilia. Otherwise known as kennel cough, this disease is highly contagious and should be vaccinated against routinely.

Coronavirus

This is usually self limiting and not life threatening. It was first noted in the late '70s about a year before parvovirus. The virus produces a yellow/brown stool and there may be depression, vomiting and diarrhea.

Lyme Disease

This was first diagnosed in the United States in 1976 in Lyme, CT in people who lived in close proximity to the deer tick. Symptoms may include acute lameness, fever, swelling of joints and loss of appetite. Your veterinarian can advise you if you live in an endemic area.

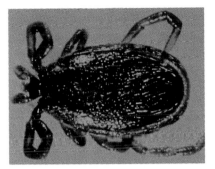

The deer tick is the most common carrier of Lyme disease. Photo courtesy of Virbac Laboratories, Inc., Fort Worth, Texas.

After your puppy has completed his puppy vaccinations, you will continue to booster the DHLPP once a year. It is customary to booster the rabies one year after the first vaccine and then, depending on where you live, it should be boostered every year or every three years. This depends on your local laws. The Lyme and corona vaccines are boostered annually and it is recommended that the bordetella be boostered every six to eight months.

ANNUAL VISIT

I would like to impress the importance of the annual check up, which would include the booster vaccinations, check for intestinal parasites and test for heartworm. Today in our very busy world it is rush, rush and see "how much you can get for how little." Unbelievably, some non-veterinary businesses have entered into the vaccination business. More harm than good can come to your dog through improper vaccinations, possibly from inferior vaccines and/or the wrong schedule. More than likely you truly care about your companion dog and over the years you have devoted much time and expense to his well being. Perhaps you are unaware that a vaccination is not just a vaccination. There is more involved. Please, please follow through with regular physical examinations. It is so important for your veterinarian to know your dog and this is especially true during middle age through the geriatric years. More than likely your older dog will require more than one physical a year. The annual physical is good preventive medicine. Through early diagnosis and subsequent treatment your dog can maintain a longer and better quality of life.

INTESTINAL PARASITES

Hookworms

These are almost microscopic intestinal worms that can cause anemia and therefore serious problems, including death, in young puppies. Hookworms can be transmitted to humans through penetration of the skin. Puppies may be born with them.

Roundworms

These are spaghetti-like worms that can cause a potbellied appearance and dull coat along with more severe symptoms, such as vomiting, diarrhea and coughing. Puppies acquire these while in the mother's uterus and through lactation. Both hookworms and roundworms may be acquired through ingestion.

Roundworm eggs, as would be seen on a fecal evaluation. The eggs must develop for at least 12 days before they are infective.

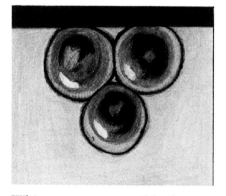

Whipworms

These have a three-month life cycle and are not acquired through the dam. They cause intermittent diarrhea usually with mucus. Whipworms are possibly the most difficult worm to eradicate. Their eggs are very resistant to most environmental factors and can last for years until the proper conditions enable them to mature. Whipworms are seldom seen in the stool.

Intestinal parasites are more prevalent in some areas than others. Climate, soil and contamination are big factors contributing to the incidence of intestinal parasites. Eggs are passed in the stool, lay on the ground and then become infective in a certain number of days. Each of the above worms has a different life cycle. Your best chance of becoming and remaining worm-free is to always pooper-scoop your yard. A fenced-in yard keeps stray dogs out, which is certainly helpful.

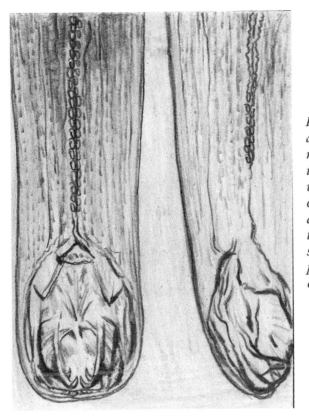

Hookworms are almost microscopic intestinal worms that can cause anemia and therefore serious problems, even death.

I would recommend having a fecal examination on your dog twice a year or more often if there is a problem. If your dog has a positive fecal sample, then he will be given the appropriate medication and you will be asked to bring back another stool sample in a certain period of time (depending on the type of worm) and then be rewormed. This process goes on until he has at least two negative samples. The different types of worms require different medications. You will be wasting your money and doing your dog an injustice by buying over-the-counter medication without first consulting your veterinarian.

OTHER INTERNAL PARASITES

Coccidiosis and Giardiasis

These protozoal infections usually affect puppies, especially in places where large numbers of puppies are brought together. Older dogs may harbor these infections but do not show signs unless they are stressed. Symptoms include diarrhea, weight loss and lack of appetite. These infections are not always apparent in the fecal examination.

Tapeworms

Seldom apparent on fecal floatation, they are diagnosed frequently as rice-like segments around the dog's anus and the base of the tail. Tapeworms are long, flat and ribbon like, sometimes several feet in length, and made up of many segments about five-eighths of an inch long. The two most common types of tapeworms found in the dog are:

(1) First the larval form of the flea tapeworm parasite must mature in an intermediate host, the flea, before it can become infective. Your dog acquires this by ingesting the flea through licking and chewing.

(2) Rabbits, rodents and certain large game animals serve as intermediate hosts for other species of tapeworms. If your dog should eat one of these infected hosts, then he can acquire tapeworms.

HEARTWORM DISEASE

This is a worm that resides in the heart and adjacent blood vessels of the lung that produces microfilaria, which circulate in the bloodstream. It is possible for a dog to be infected with any number of worms from one to a hundred that can be 6 to 14 inches long. It is a life-threatening disease, expensive to treat and easily prevented.

Depending on where you live, your veterinarian may recommend a preventive year-round and either an annual or semiannual blood test. The most common preventive is given once a month.

Dirofilaria—adult worms in the heart of a dog. It is possible for a dog to be infected with any number of worms that can be 6 to 14 inches long. Courtesy of Merck AgVet.

118

Fleas can cause an allergic reaction in your dog. If your Beagle seems to be scratching excessively, check his coat thoroughly for parasites.

EXTERNAL PARASITES

Fleas

These pests are not only the dog's worst enemy but also enemy to the owner's pocketbook. Preventing is less expensive than treating, but regardless we'd prefer to spend our money elsewhere. Likely, the majority of our dogs are allergic to the bite of a flea, and in many cases it only takes one flea bite. The protein in the flea's saliva is the culprit. Allergic dogs have a reaction, which usually results in a "hot spot." More than likely such a reaction will involve a trip to the veterinarian for treatment. Yes, prevention is less expensive. Fortunately today there are several good products available.

If there is a flea infestation, no one product is going to correct the problem. Not only will the dog require treatment so will the environment. In general flea collars are not very effective although there is now available an "egg" collar that will kill the eggs on the dog. Dips are the most economical but they are messy. There are some effective shampoos and treatments available through pet shops and veterinarians. An oral tablet arrived on the American market in 1995 and was popular in Europe the previous year. It sterilizes the female flea but will not kill adult fleas. Therefore the tablet, which is given monthly, will decrease the flea population but is not a "cure-all." Those dogs that suffer from flea-bite allergy will still be subjected to the bite of the flea. Another popular parasiticide is permethrin, which is applied to the back of the dog in one or two places depending on the dog's weight. This product works as a repellent causing the flea to get "hot feet" and jump off. Do not confuse this product with some of the organophosphates that are also applied to the dog's back.

Because the Beagle has long ears that fold over, be sure to keep them clean and check them regularly for infections.

Some products are not usable on young puppies. Treating fleas should be done under your veterinarian's guidance. Frequently it is necessary to combine products and the layman does not have the knowledge

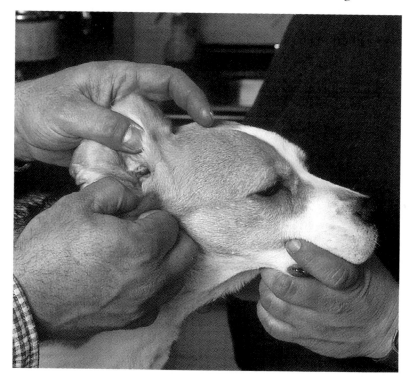

regarding possible toxicities. It is hard to believe but there are a few dogs that do have a natural resistance to fleas. Nevertheless it would be wise to treat all pets at the same time. Don't forget your cats. Cats just love to prowl the neighborhood and consequently return with unwanted guests.

The cat flea is the most common flea of both cats and dogs. Courtesy of Fleabusters, Rx for Fleas, Inc., Fort Lauderdale, Florida.

Adult fleas live on the dog but their eggs drop off the dog into the environment. There they go through four larval stages before reaching adulthood, and thereby are able to jump back on the poor unsuspecting dog. The cycle resumes and takes between 21 to 28 days under ideal conditions. There are environmental products available that will kill both the adult fleas and the larvae.

Ticks

Ticks carry Rocky Mountain Spotted Fever, Lyme disease and can cause tick paralysis. They should be removed with tweezers, trying to pull out the head. The jaws carry disease. There is a tick preventive collar that does an excellent job. The ticks automatically back out on those dogs wearing collars.

Sarcoptic Mange

This is a mite that is difficult to find on skin scrapings. The pinnal reflex is a good indicator of this disease. Rub the ends of the pinna (ear) together and the dog will start scratching with his foot. Sarcoptes are highly contagious to other dogs and to humans although they do not live long on humans. They cause intense itching.

Demodectic Mange

This is a mite that is passed from the dam to her puppies. It affects youngsters age three to ten months. Diagnosis is confirmed by skin scraping. Small areas of alopecia around the eyes, lips and/or forelegs become visible. There is little itching unless there is a secondary bacterial infection. Some breeds are afflicted more than others.

Cheyletiella

This causes intense itching and is diagnosed by skin scraping. It lives in the outer layers of the skin of dogs, cats, rabbits and humans. Yellow-gray scales may be found on the back and the rump, top of the head and the nose.

TO BREED OR NOT TO BREED

More than likely your breeder has requested that you have your puppy neutered or spayed. Your breeder's request is based on what is healthiest for your dog and what is most beneficial for your breed. Experienced and conscientious breeders devote many years into developing a bloodline. In order to do this, he makes every effort to plan each breeding in regard to conformation, temperament and health. This type of breeder does his best to perform the necessary testing (i.e., OFA, CERF, testing for inherited blood disorders, thyroid, etc.).

By breeding only the best quality dogs, good health and temperament are passed down to each generation.

Spaying/neutering is often the best option for your family pet. The health benefits are numerous and it minimizes the risk for certain diseases.

Testing is expensive and sometimes very disheartening when a favorite dog doesn't pass his health tests. The health history pertains not only to the breeding stock but to the immediate ancestors. Reputable breeders do not want their offspring to be bred indiscriminately. Therefore you may be asked to neuter or spay your puppy. Of course there is always the exception, and your breeder may agree to let you breed your dog under his direct supervision. This is an important concept. More and more effort is being made to breed healthier dogs.

Spay/Neuter

There are numerous benefits of performing this surgery at six months of age. Unspayed females are subject to mammary and ovarian cancer. In order to prevent mammary cancer she must be spayed prior to her first heat cycle. Later in life, an unspayed female may develop a pyometra (an infected uterus), which is definitely life threatening.

Spaying is performed under a general anesthetic and is easy on the young dog. As you might expect it is a little harder on the older dog, but that is no reason to deny her the surgery.

The surgery removes the ovaries and uterus. It is important to remove all the ovarian tissue. If some is left behind, she could remain attractive to males. In order to view the ovaries, a reasonably long incision is necessary. An ovariohysterectomy is considered major surgery.

The Beagle is a generally healthy dog and, when loved and well cared for, will live a long and fruitful life.

Neutering the male at a young age will inhibit some characteristic male behavior that owners frown upon. Some boys will not hike their legs and mark territory if they are neutered at six months of age. Also neutering at a young age has hormonal benefits, lessening the chance of hormonal aggressiveness.

Surgery involves removing the testicles but leaving the scrotum. If there should be a retained testicle, then he definitely needs to be neutered before the age of two or three years. Retained testicles can develop into cancer. Unneutered males are at risk for testicular cancer, perineal fistulas, perianal tumors and fistulas and prostatic disease.

Intact males and females are prone to housebreaking accidents. Females urinate frequently before, during and after heat cycles, and males tend to mark territory if there is a female in heat. Males may show the same behavior if there is a visiting dog or guests.

Surgery involves a sterile operating procedure equivalent to human surgery. The incision site is shaved, surgically scrubbed and draped. The veterinarian wears a sterile surgical gown, cap, mask and gloves. Anesthesia should be monitored by a registered technician. It is customary for the veterinarian to recommend a pre-anesthetic blood screening, looking for metabolic problems and a ECG rhythm strip to check for normal heart function. Today anesthetics are equal to human anesthetics, which enables your dog to walk out of the clinic the same day as surgery.

Some folks worry about their dog gaining weight after being neutered or spayed. This is usually not the case. It is true that some dogs may be less active so they could develop a problem, but most dogs are just as active as they were before surgery. However, if your dog should begin to gain, then you need to decrease his food and see to it that he gets a little more exercise.

DENTAL CARE for Your Dog's Life

So you've got a new puppy! You also have a new set of puppy teeth in your household. Anyone who has ever raised a puppy is abundantly aware of these new teeth. Your puppy will chew anything it can reach, chase your shoelaces, and play "tear the rag" with any piece of clothing it can find. When puppies are newly born, they have no teeth. At about four weeks of age, puppies of most breeds begin to develop their deciduous or baby teeth. They begin eating semi-solid food, fighting and biting with their litter mates, and learning discipline from their mother. As their new teeth come in, they inflict more pain on their mother's breasts, so her feeding sessions become less frequent and shorter. By six or eight weeks, the mother will start growling to warn her pups when they are fighting too roughly or hurting her as they nurse too much with their new teeth.

Puppies need to chew. It is a necessary part of their physical and mental development. They develop muscles and necessary life skills as they drag objects around, fight over possession, and vocalize alerts and warnings. Puppies chew on things to explore their world. They are using their sense of taste to determine what is food and what is not. How else can they tell an electrical cord from a lizard? At about four months of age, most puppies begin shedding their baby teeth. Often these

Carrots are rich in fiber, carbohydrates and vitamin A. The Carrot Bone™ by Nylabone® is a durable chew containing no

plastics or artificial ingredients and it can be served to your Beagle as-is, in bone-hard form, or microwaved to a biscuity consistency.

teeth need some help
to come out and make
way for the permanent
teeth. The incisors
(front teeth) will be
replaced first. Then,
the adult canine or fang
teeth erupt. When the
baby tooth is not shed
before the permanent
tooth comes in,
veterinarians call it a
retained deciduous
tooth. This condition

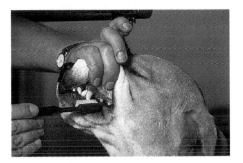

*Brushing your dog's teeth regularly
will help prevent tooth decay and
periodontal disease.*

will often cause gum infections by trapping hair and debris
between the permanent tooth and the retained baby tooth.
Nylafloss® is an excellent device for puppies to use. They can
toss it, drag it, and chew on the many surfaces it presents. The
baby teeth can catch in the nylon material, aiding in their
removal. Puppies that have adequate chew toys will have less
destructive behavior, develop more physically, and have less
chance of retained deciduous teeth.

During the first year, your dog should be seen by your
veterinarian at regular intervals. Your veterinarian will let you
know when to bring in your puppy for vaccinations and
parasite examinations. At each visit, your veterinarian should
inspect the lips, teeth, and mouth as part of a complete
physical examination. You should take some part in the
maintenance of your dog's oral health. You should examine
your dog's mouth weekly throughout his first year to make
sure there are no sores, foreign objects, tooth problems, etc. If
your dog drools excessively, shakes its head, or has bad breath,
consult your veterinarian. By the time your dog is six months
old, the permanent teeth are all in and plaque can start to
accumulate on the tooth surfaces. This is when your dog needs
to develop good dental-care habits to prevent calculus build-up
on its teeth. Brushing is best. That is a fact that cannot be
denied. However, some dogs do not like their teeth brushed
regularly, or you may not be able to accomplish the task. In
that case, you should consider a product that will help prevent
plaque and calculus build-up.

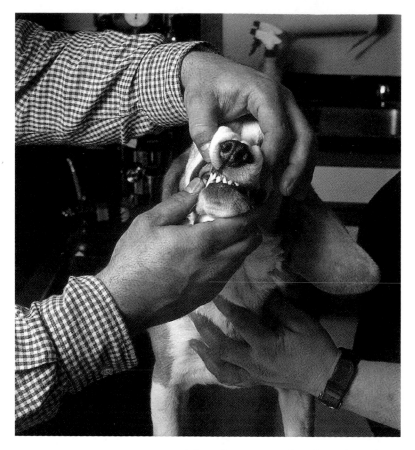

A thorough oral exam should be a part of your annual veterinary check-up.

The Plaque Attackers® and Galileo Bone® are other excellent choices for the first three years of a dog's life. Their shapes make them interesting for the dog. As the dog chews on them, the solid polyurethane massages the gums which improves the blood circulation to the periodontal tissues. Projections on the chew devices increase the surface and are in contact with the tooth for more efficient cleaning. The unique shape and consistency prevent your dog from exerting excessive force on his own teeth or from breaking off pieces of the bone. If your dog is an aggressive chewer or weighs more than 55 pounds (25 kg), you should consider giving him a Nylabone®, the most durable chew product on the market.

The Gumabones ®, made by the Nylabone Company, is constructed of strong polyurethane, which is softer than nylon. Less powerful chewers prefer the Gumabones® to the Nylabones®. A super option for your dog is the Hercules Bone®, a uniquely shaped bone named after the great Olympian for its exception strength. Like all Nylabone products, they are specially scented to make them attractive to your dog. Ask your veterinarian about these bones and he will validate the good doctor's prescription: Nylabones® not only give your dog a good chewing workout but also help to save your dog's teeth (and even his life, as it protects him from possible fatal periodontal diseases).

In order to satisfy your Beagle's urge to chew, give him the Gumabone® Wishbone. It is made of non-toxic polyurethane and the chewed ends break up plaque.

By the time dogs are four years old, 75% of them have periodontal disease. It is the most common infection in dogs. Yearly examinations by your veterinarian are essential to maintaining your dog's good health. If your veterinarian detects periodontal disease, he or she may recommend a prophylactic cleaning. To do a thorough cleaning, it will be necessary to put your dog under anesthesia. With modern gas anesthetics and monitoring equipment, the procedure is pretty safe. Your veterinarian will scale the teeth with an ultrasound scaler or hand instrument. This removes the calculus from the teeth. If there are calculus deposits below the gum line, the veterinarian will plane the roots to make them smooth. After all of the calculus has been removed, the teeth are polished with pumice in a polishing cup. If any medical or surgical treatment is needed, it is done at this time. The final step would be fluoride treatment and your follow-up treatment at home. If the periodontal disease is advanced, the veterinarian may prescribe a medicated mouth rinse or antibiotics for use at home. Make sure your dog has safe, clean and attractive chew toys and treats. Chooz® treats are another way of using a consumable treat to help keep your dog's teeth clean.

Rawhide is the most popular of all materials for a dog to chew. This has never been good news to dog owners, because rawhide is inherently very dangerous for dogs. Thousands of dogs have died from rawhide, having swallowed the hide after it has become soft and mushy, only to cause stomach and intestinal blockage. A new rawhide product on the market has finally solved the problem of rawhide: molded Roar-Hide® from Nylabone. These are composed of processed, *If your Beagle would rather chew than do anything, give him a Gumabone®.* cut up, and melted American rawhide injected into your dog's favorite shape: a dog bone. These dog-safe devices smell and taste like rawhide but don't break up. The ridges on the bones help to fight tartar build-up on the teeth and they last ten times longer than the usual rawhide chews.

As your dog ages, professional examination and cleaning should become more frequent. The mouth should be inspected at least once a year. Your veterinarian may recommend visits every six months. In the geriatric patient, organs such as the heart, liver, and kidneys do not function as well as when they were young. Your veterinarian will probably want to test these organs' functions prior to using general anesthesia for dental cleaning. If your dog is a good chewer and you work closely with your veterinarian, your dog can keep all of its teeth all of its life. However, as your dog ages, his sense of smell, sight, and taste will diminish. He may not have the desire to chase, trap or chew his toys. He will also not have the energy to chew for long periods, as arthritis and periodontal disease make chewing painful. This will leave you with more responsibility for keeping his teeth clean and healthy. The dog that would not let you brush his teeth at one year of age, may let you brush his teeth now that he is ten years old.

If you train your dog with good chewing habits as a puppy, he will have healthier teeth throughout his life.

Nylafloss® is a great tug toy for your Beagle and it does wonders for the young puppy's emerging new teeth.

TRAVELING with Your Beagle

The earlier you start traveling with your new puppy or dog, the better. He needs to become accustomed to traveling. However, some dogs are nervous riders and become carsick easily. It is helpful if he starts with an empty stomach. Do not despair, as it will go better if you continue taking him with you on short fun rides. How would you feel if every time you rode in the car you stopped at the doctor's for an injection? You would soon dread that nasty car. Older dogs that tend to get carsick may have more of a problem adjusting to traveling. Those dogs that are having a serious problem may benefit from some medication prescribed by the veterinarian.

Do give your dog a chance to relieve himself before getting into the car. It is a good idea to be prepared for a clean up with a leash, paper towels, bag and terry cloth towel.

The safest place for your dog is in a fiberglass crate, although close confinement can promote carsickness in some dogs. If your dog is nervous you can try letting him ride on the seat next to you or in someone's lap.

An alternative to the crate would be to use a car harness made for dogs and/or a safety strap attached to the harness or collar. Whatever you do, do not let your dog ride in the back of a pickup truck unless he is securely tied on a very short lead.

The more you bring your dog on outings with you, the more willing he will be to tag along. These two guys take a snooze after a romp in the park.

I've seen trucks stop quickly and, even though the dog was tied, it fell out and was dragged.

Another advantage of the crate is that it is a safe place to leave him if you need to run into the store. Otherwise you wouldn't be able to leave the windows down. Keep in mind that while many dogs are overly protective in their crates, this may not be enough to deter dognappers. In some states it is against the law to leave a dog in the car unattended.

If you accustom your Beagle to traveling early in life, you'll never have to leave him at home. Benny, owned by DJ Queenan, waits patiently for his master's arrival.

Because they are such accommodating dogs, Beagles can make themselves at home anywhere. These three enjoy a day at the beach.

Never leave a dog loose in the car wearing a collar and leash. More than one dog has killed himself by hanging. Do not let him put his head out an open window. Foreign debris can be blown into his eyes. When leaving your dog unattended in a car, consider the temperature. It can take less than five minutes to reach temperatures over 100 degrees Fahrenheit.

This basketful of Whisperfield puppies are all packed up and ready to go!

TRIPS

Perhaps you are taking a trip. Give consideration to what is best for your dog—traveling with you or boarding. When traveling by car, van or motor home, you need to think ahead about locking your vehicle. In all probability you have many valuables in the car and do not wish to leave it unlocked. Perhaps most valuable and not replaceable is your dog. Give thought to securing your vehicle and providing adequate ventilation for him. Another consideration for you when traveling with your dog is medical problems that may arise and little inconveniences, such as exposure to external parasites. Some areas of the country are quite flea infested. You may want to carry flea spray with you. This is even a good idea when staying in motels. Quite possibly you are not the only occupant of the room.

Unbelievably many motels and even hotels do allow canine guests, even some very first-class ones. Gaines Pet Foods Corporation publishes *Touring With Towser*, a directory of domestic hotels and motels that accommodate guests with dogs. Their address is Gaines TWT, PO Box 5700, Kankakee, IL, 60902. Call ahead to any motel that you may be considering and see if they accept pets. Sometimes it is necessary to pay a deposit against room damage. The management may feel reassured if you mention that your dog will be crated. If you do travel with your dog, take along plenty of baggies so that you can clean up after him. When we all do our share in cleaning up, we make it possible for motels to continue accepting our pets. As a matter of fact, you should practice cleaning up everywhere you take your dog.

Beagles who travel often, like show dogs, come to enjoy the ever-changing life on the road.

If you travel with your Beagle, make sure you bring a familiar toy or blanket to make him feel at home.

Depending on where your are traveling, you may need an up-to-date health certificate issued by your veterinarian. It is good policy to take along your dog's medical information, which would include the name, address and phone number of your veterinarian, vaccination record, rabies certificate, and any medication he is taking.

AIR TRAVEL

When traveling by air, you need to contact the airlines to check their policy. Usually you have to make arrangements up to a couple of weeks in advance for traveling with your dog. The airlines require your dog to travel in an airline approved fiberglass crate. Usually these can be purchased through the airlines but they are also readily available in most pet-supply stores. If your dog is not accustomed to a crate, then it is a good idea to get him acclimated to it before your trip. The day of the actual trip you should withhold water about one hour ahead of departure and no food for about 12 hours. The airlines generally have temperature restrictions, which do not allow pets to travel if it is either too cold or too hot. Frequently these restrictions are based on the temperatures at the departure and arrival airports. It's best to inquire about a health certificate. These usually need to be issued within ten days of departure. You should arrange for non-stop, direct flights and if a commuter plane should be involved, check to see if it will carry dogs. Some don't. The Humane Society of the United States has put together a tip sheet for airline traveling. You can receive a copy by sending a self-addressed stamped envelope to:

The Humane Society of the United States
Tip Sheet
2100 L Street NW
Washington, DC 20037.

Boarding your dog in a kennel is one option if your must leave him overnight for any length of time.

Regulations differ for traveling outside of the country and are sometimes changed without notice. Well in advance you need to write or call the appropriate consulate or agricultural department for instructions. Some countries have lengthy quarantines (six months), and countries differ in their rabies vaccination requirements. For instance, it may have to be given at least 30 days ahead of your departure.

Do make sure your dog is wearing proper identification including your name, phone number and city. You never know when you might be in an accident and separated from your dog. Or your dog could be frightened and somehow manage to escape and run away.

Another suggestion would be to carry in-case-of-emergency instructions. These would include the address and phone number of a relative or friend, your veterinarian's name, address and phone number, and your dog's medical information.

BOARDING KENNELS

Perhaps you have decided that you need to board your dog. Your veterinarian can recommend a good boarding facility or possibly a pet sitter that will come to your house. It is customary for the boarding kennel to ask for proof of vaccination for the DHLPP, rabies and bordetella vaccine.

A reputable boarding kennel will require that every dog that stays with them is up to date with his vaccinations.

The bordetella should have been given within six months of boarding. This is for your protection. If they do not ask for this proof I would not board at their kennel. Ask about flea control. Those dogs that suffer flea-bite allergy can get in trouble at a boarding kennel. Unfortunately boarding kennels are limited on how much they are able to do.

For more information on pet sitting, contact NAPPS:
National Association of Professional Pet Sitters
1200 G Street, NW
Suite 760
Washington, DC 20005.

Some pet clinics have technicians that pet sit and technicians that board clinic patients in their homes. This may be an alternative for you. Ask your veterinarian if they have an employee that can help you. There is a definite advantage of having a technician care for your dog, especially if your dog is on medication or is a senior citizen.

You can write for a copy of *Traveling With Your Pet* from ASPCA, Education Department, 441 E. 92nd Street, New York, NY 10128.

Ready for a morning spin around the block...

IDENTIFICATION and Finding the Lost Dog

There are several ways of identifying your dog. The old standby is a collar with dog license, rabies, and ID tags. Unfortunately collars have a way of being separated from the dog and tags fall off. We're not suggesting you shouldn't use a collar and tags. If they stay intact and on the dog, they are the quickest way of identification.

For several years owners have been tattooing their dogs. Some tattoos use a number with a registry. Here lies the problem because there are several registries to check. If you wish to tattoo, use your social security number. The humane shelters have the means to trace it. It is usually done on

The newest method of identification is microchipping. The microchip is a computer chip that is no bigger than a grain of rice.

Because they tend to wander off, every Beagle owner should have a securely fenced-in yard.

the inside of the rear thigh. The area is first shaved and numbed. There is no pain, although a few dogs do not like the buzzing sound. Occasionally tattooing is not legible and needs to be redone.

The newest method of identification is microchipping. The microchip is a computer chip that is no larger than a grain of rice. The veterinarian implants it by injection between the shoulder blades. The dog feels no discomfort. If your dog is lost and picked up by the humane society, they can trace you by scanning the microchip, which has its own code. Microchip scanners are friendly to other brands of microchips and their registries. The microchip comes with a dog tag saying the dog is microchipped. It is the safest way of identifying your dog.

FINDING THE LOST DOG

I am sure you will agree that there would be little worse than losing your dog. Responsible pet owners rarely lose their dogs. They do not let their dogs run free because they don't want harm to come to them. Not only that but in most, if not all, states there is a leash law.

Beware of fenced-in yards. They can be a hazard. Dogs find ways to escape either over or under the fence. Another fast exit is through the gate that perhaps the neighbor's child left unlocked.

Losing your beloved Beagle is a nightmare you'll never want to face. Take every precaution to avoid it.

Below is a list that hopefully will be of help to you if you need it. Remember don't give up, keep looking. Your dog is worth your efforts.

1. Contact your neighbors and put flyers with a photo on it in their mailboxes. Information you should include would be the dog's name, breed, sex, color, age, source of identification, when your dog was last seen and where, and your name and phone numbers. It may be helpful to say the dog needs medical care. Offer a *reward*.

2. Check all local shelters daily. It is also possible for your dog to be picked up away from home and end up in an out-of-the-way shelter. Check these too. Go in person. It is not good enough to call. Most shelters are limited on the time they can hold dogs then they are put up for adoption or euthanized. There is the possibility that your dog will not make it to the shelter for several days. Your dog could have been wandering or someone may have tried to keep him.

3. Notify all local veterinarians. Call and send flyers.

4. Call your breeder. Frequently breeders are contacted when one of their breed is found.

5. Contact the rescue group for your breed.

6. Contact local schools—children may have seen your dog.

7. Post flyers at the schools, groceries, gas stations, convenience stores, veterinary clinics, groomers and any other place that will allow them.

8. Advertise in the newspaper.

9. Advertise on the radio.

BEHAVIOR and Canine Communication

Studies of the human/animal bond point out the importance of the unique relationships that exist between people and their pets. Those of us who share our lives with pets understand the special part they play through companionship, service and protection. For many, the pet/owner bond goes beyond simple companionship; pets are often considered members of the family. A leading pet food manufacturer recently conducted a nationwide survey of pet owners to gauge just how important pets were in their lives. Here's what they found:

- 76 percent allow their pets to sleep on their beds
- 78 percent think of their pets as their children
- 84 percent display photos of their pets, mostly in their homes
- 84 percent think that their pets react to their own emotions
- 100 percent talk to their pets
- 97 percent think that their pets understand what they're saying

Are you surprised?

Senior citizens show more concern for their own eating habits when they have the responsibility of feeding a dog. Seeing that their dog is routinely exercised encourages the owner to think of schedules that otherwise may seem unimportant to the senior citizen. The older owner may be arthritic and feeling poorly but with responsibility

Well-bred Beagles in the great outdoors—a sportsman's dream.

144

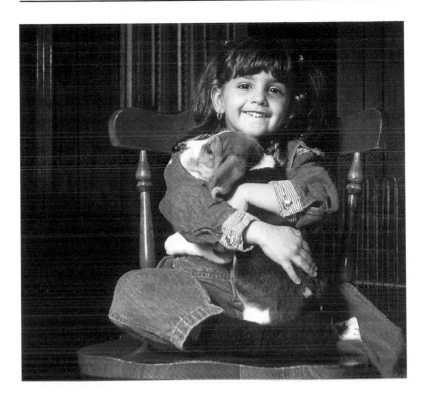

Children make great playmates for your Beagle, and dog ownership can teach a child responsibility and respect for animals.

for his dog he has a reason to get up and get moving. It is a big plus if his dog is an attention seeker who will demand such from his owner.

Over the last couple of decades, it has been shown that pets relieve the stress of those who lead busy lives. Owning a pet has been known to lessen the occurrence of heart attack and stroke.

Many single folks thrive on the companionship of a dog. Lifestyles are very different from a long time ago, and today more individuals seek the single life. However, they receive fulfillment from owning a dog.

Most likely the majority of our dogs live in family environments. The companionship they provide is well worth the effort involved. In my opinion, every child should have the opportunity to have a family dog. Dogs teach responsibility through understanding their care, feelings and even respecting their life cycles. Frequently those children who have not been exposed to dogs grow up afraid of dogs, which isn't good. Dogs sense timidity and some will take advantage of the situation.

Today more dogs are serving as service dogs. Since the origination of the Seeing Eye dogs years ago, we now have trained hearing dogs. Also dogs are trained to provide service for the handicapped and are able to perform many different tasks for their owners. Search and Rescue dogs, with their handlers, are sent throughout the world to assist in recovery of disaster victims. They are life savers.

Therapy dogs are very popular with nursing homes, and some hospitals even allow them to visit. The inhabitants truly look forward to their visits. They wanted and were allowed to have visiting dogs in their beds to hold and love.

Nationally there is a Pet Awareness Week to educate students and others about the value and basic care of our pets. Many

Can Beagles really do anything? Londonderry's Paul Oliver is ready to lend a paw to Santa's reindeers.

countries take an even greater interest in their pets than Americans do. In those countries the pets are allowed to accompany their owners into restaurants and shops, etc. In the U.S. this freedom is only available to our service dogs. Even so we think very highly of the human/animal bond.

CANINE BEHAVIOR

Canine behavior problems are the number-one reason for pet owners to dispose of their dogs, either through new homes, humane shelters or euthanasia. Unfortunately there are too many owners who are unwilling to devote the necessary time to properly train their dogs. On the other hand, there are those who not only are concerned about inherited health problems but are also aware of the dog's mental stability.

Beagle puppies are gregarious and curious.

You may realize that a breed and his group relatives (i.e., sporting, hounds, etc.) show tendencies to behavioral characteristics. An experienced breeder can acquaint you with his breed's personality. Unfortunately many breeds are labeled with poor temperaments when actually the breed as a whole is not affected but only a small percentage of individuals within the breed.

Inheritance and environment contribute to the dog's behavior. Some naïve people suggest inbreeding as the cause of bad temperaments. Inbreeding only results in poor behavior if the ancestors carry the trait. If there are excellent temperaments behind the dogs, then inbreeding will promote good temperaments in the offspring. Did you ever consider that inbreeding is what sets the characteristics of a breed? A purebred dog is the end result of inbreeding. This does not spare the mixed-breed dog from the same problems. Mixed-breed dogs frequently are the offspring of purebred dogs.

Not too many decades ago most of our dogs led a different lifestyle than what is prevalent today. Usually mom stayed home so the dog had human companionship and someone to discipline it if needed. Not much was expected from the dog. Today's mom works and everyone's life is at a much faster pace.

The dog may have to adjust to being a "weekend" dog. The family is gone all day during the week, and the dog is left to his own devices for entertainment. Some dogs sleep all day waiting for their family to come home and others become wigwam wreckers if given the opportunity. Crates do ensure the safety of the dog and the house. However, he could become a physically and emotionally cripple if he doesn't get enough exercise and attention. We still appreciate and

Socialization with littermates is very important to your Beagle's personality development.

want the companionship of our dogs although we expect more from them. In many cases we tend to forget dogs are just that—*dogs* not human beings.

SOCIALIZING AND TRAINING

Many prospective puppy buyers lack experience regarding the proper socialization and training needed to develop the type of pet we all desire. In the first 18 months, training does take some work. It is easier to start proper training before there is a problem that needs to be corrected.

The initial work begins with the breeder. The breeder should start socializing the puppy at five to six weeks of age and cannot let up. Human socializing is critical up through 12 weeks of age and likewise important during the following months. The litter should be left together during the first few weeks but it is necessary to separate them by ten weeks of age. Leaving them together after that time will increase competition for litter dominance. If puppies are not socialized with people by 12 weeks of age, they will be timid in later life.

Introduced early enough, a Beagle can happily co-exist with other pets. This guy doesn't seem to mind friends hanging around his house.

The eight- to ten-week age period is a fearful time for puppies. They need to be handled very gently around children and adults. There should be no harsh discipline during this time. Starting at 14 weeks of age, the puppy begins the juvenile period, which ends when he reaches sexual maturity around six to 14 months of age.

During the juvenile period he needs to be introduced to strangers (adults, children and other dogs) on the home property. At sexual maturity he will begin to bark at strangers and become more protective. Males start to lift their legs to urinate but if you desire you can inhibit this behavior by walking your boy on leash away from trees, shrubs, fences, etc.

Perhaps you are thinking about an older puppy. You need to inquire about the puppy's social experience. If he has lived in a kennel, he may have a hard time adjusting to people and environmental stimuli. Assuming he has had a good social upbringing, there are advantages to an older puppy.

Training includes puppy kindergarten and a minimum of one to two basic training classes. During these classes you will learn how to dominate your youngster. This is especially important if you own a large breed of dog. It is somewhat harder, if not nearly impossible, for some owners to be the Alpha figure when their dog towers over them. You will be taught how to properly restrain your dog. This concept is important. Again it puts you in the Alpha position. All dogs need to be restrained many times during their lives. Believe it or not, some of our worst offenders are the eight-week-old puppies that are brought to our clinic. They need to be gently restrained for a nail trim but the way they carry on you would think we were killing them. In comparison, their vaccination is a "piece of cake." When we ask dogs to do something that is not agreeable to them, then their worst comes out. Life will be easier for your dog if you expose him at a young age to the necessities of life—proper behavior and restraint.

Understanding the Dog's Language

Most authorities agree that the dog is a descendent of the wolf. The dog and wolf have similar traits. For instance both are pack oriented and prefer not to be isolated for long periods

A properly socialized Beagle makes friends wherever he goes!

of time. Another characteristic is that the dog, like the wolf, looks to the leader—Alpha—for direction. Both the wolf and the dog communicate through body language, not only within their pack but with outsiders.

Every pack has an Alpha figure. The dog looks to you, or should look to you, to be that leader. If your dog doesn't receive the proper training and guidance, he very well may replace you as

Are these the faces of mischief makers? This pair of naughty Beagles was caught in the act and couldn't look more contrite.

Bellevue Blossom dreams of fun times in the field but appreciates the comfort of her favorite chair.

Alpha. This would be a serious problem and is certainly a disservice to your dog.

Eye contact is one way the Alpha wolf keeps order within his pack. You are Alpha so you must establish eye contact with your puppy. Obviously your puppy will have to look at you. Practice eye contact even if you need to hold his head for five to ten seconds at a time. You can give him a treat as a reward. Make sure your eye contact is gentle and not threatening. Later, if he has been naughty, it is permissible to give him a long, penetrating look. There are some older dogs that never learned eye contact as puppies and cannot accept eye contact. You should avoid eye contact with these dogs since they feel threatened and will retaliate as such.

BODY LANGUAGE

The play bow, when the forequarters are down and the hindquarters are elevated, is an invitation to play. Puppies play fight, which helps them learn the acceptable limits of biting. This is necessary for later in their lives. Nevertheless, an owner may be falsely reassured by the playful nature of his dog's aggression. Playful aggression toward another dog or human may be an indication of serious aggression in the future. Owners should never play fight or play tug-of-war with any dog that is inclined to be dominant.

Signs of submission are:
1. Avoids eye contact.
2. Active submission—the dog crouches down, ears back and the tail is lowered.
3. Passive submission—the dog rolls on his side with his hindlegs in the air and frequently urinates.

Signs of dominance are:
1. Makes eye contact.
2. Stands with ears up, tail up and the hair raised on his neck.
3. Shows dominance over another dog by standing at right angles over it.

Dominant dogs tend to behave in characteristic ways such as:
1. The dog may be unwilling to move from his place (i.e., reluctant to give up the sofa if the owner wants to sit there).
2. He may not part with toys or objects in his mouth and may show possessiveness with his food bowl.
3. He may not respond quickly to commands.
4. He may be disagreeable for grooming and dislikes to be petted.

Dogs are popular because of their sociable nature. Those that have contact with humans during the first 12 weeks of life regard them as a member of their own species—their pack. All dogs have the potential for both dominant and submissive behavior. Only through experience and training do they learn to whom it is appropriate to show which behavior. Not all dogs are concerned with dominance but owners need to be aware of that potential. It is wise for the owner to establish his dominance early on.

A human can express dominance or submission toward a dog in the following ways:

1. Meeting the dog's gaze signals dominance. Averting the gaze signals submission. If the dog growls or threatens, averting the gaze is the first avoiding action to take—it may prevent attack. It is important to establish eye contact in the puppy. The

This Beagle shows submission to her owner—and gets an enjoyable belly rub!

older dog that has not been exposed to eye contact may see it as a threat and will not be willing to submit.

2. Being taller than the dog signals dominance; being lower signals submission. This is why, when attempting to make friends with a strange dog or catch the runaway, one should kneel down to his level. Some owners see their dogs become dominant when allowed on the furniture or on the bed. Then he is at the owner's level.

3. An owner can gain dominance by ignoring all the dog's social initiatives. The owner pays attention to the dog only when he obeys a command.

No dog should be allowed to achieve dominant status over any adult or child. Ways of preventing are as follows:

1. Handle the puppy gently, especially during the three- to four-month period.

2. Let the children and adults handfeed him and teach him to take food without lunging or grabbing.

3. Do not allow him to chase children or joggers.

4. Do not allow him to jump on people or mount their legs. Even females may be inclined to mount. It is not only a male habit.

5. Do not allow him to growl for any reason.

6. Don't participate in wrestling or tug-of-war games.

7. Don't physically punish puppies for aggressive behavior. Restrain him from repeating the infraction and teach an alternative behavior. Dogs should earn everything they receive from their owners. This would include sitting to receive petting or treats, sitting before going out the door and sitting to receive the collar and leash. These types of exercises reinforce the owner's dominance.

Young children should never be left alone with a dog. It is important that children learn some basic obedience commands so they have some control over the dog. They will gain the respect of their dog.

You can tell a puppy's personality by watching him react to different situations. This shy guy doesn't want to leave his master's side for a minute.

Squiggles demonstrates the agility and dexterity of the Beagle by flying over the bar jump.

FEAR

One of the most common problems dogs experience is being fearful. Some dogs are more afraid than others. On the lesser side, which is sometimes humorous to watch, dogs can be afraid of a strange object. They act silly when something is out of place in the house. We call his problem perceptive intelligence. He realizes the abnormal within his known environment. He does not react the same way in strange environments since he does not know what is normal.

On the more serious side is a fear of people. This can result in backing off, seeking his own space and saying "leave me alone" or it can result in an aggressive behavior that may lead to challenging the person. Respect that the dog wants to be left alone and give him time to come forward. If you approach the cornered dog, he may resort to snapping. If you leave him alone, he may decide to come forward, which should be rewarded with a treat.

Some dogs may initially be too fearful to take treats. In these cases it is helpful to make sure the dog hasn't eaten for about 24 hours. Being a little hungry encourages him to accept the treats, especially if they are of the "gourmet" variety.

Dogs can be afraid of numerous things, including loud noises and thunderstorms. Invariably the owner rewards (by comforting) the dog when it shows signs of fearfulness. When your dog is frightened, direct his attention to something else and act happy. Don't dwell on his fright.

"The dog as art." Hermann J. Mueller Beagles buddies create a canine tableau vivant.

AGGRESSION

Some different types of aggression are: predatory, defensive, dominance, possessive, protective, fear induced, noise provoked, "rage" syndrome (unprovoked aggression), maternal and aggression directed toward other dogs. Aggression is the most common behavioral problem encountered. Protective breeds are expected to be more aggressive than others but with the proper upbringing they can make very dependable companions. You need to be able to read your dog.

Many factors contribute to aggression including genetics and environment. An improper environment, which may include the living conditions, lack of social life, excessive punishment, being attacked or frightened by an aggressive dog, etc., can all influence a dog's behavior. Even spoiling him and giving too much praise may be detrimental. Isolation and the lack of human contact or exposure to frequent teasing by children or adults also can ruin a good dog.

Lack of direction, fear, or confusion lead to aggression in those dogs that are so inclined. Any obedience exercise, even the sit and down, can direct the dog and overcome fear and/or confusion. Every dog should learn these commands as a youngster, and there should be periodic reinforcement.

When a dog is showing signs of aggression, you should speak calmly (no screaming or hysterics) and firmly give a command that he understands, such as the sit. As soon as your dog obeys, you have assumed your dominant position. Aggression presents a problem because there may be danger to others. Sometimes it is an emotional issue. Owners may consciously or unconsciously encourage their dog's aggression. Other owners show

responsibility by accepting the problem and taking measures to keep it under control. The owner is responsible for his dog's actions, and it is not wise to take a chance on someone being bitten, especially a child. Euthanasia is the solution for some owners and in severe cases this may be the best choice. However, few dogs are that dangerous and very few are that much of a threat to their owners. If caution is exercised and professional help is gained early on, most cases can be controlled.

Some authorities recommend feeding a lower protein (less than 20 percent) diet. They believe this can aid in reducing aggression. If the dog loses weight, then vegetable oil can be added. Veterinarians and behaviorists are having some success with pharmacology. In many cases treatment is possible and can improve the situation.

If you have done everything according to "the book" regarding training and socializing and are still having a behavior problem, don't procrastinate. It is important that the problem gets attention before it is out of hand. It is estimated that 20 percent of a veterinarian's time may be devoted to dealing with problems before they become so intolerable that the dog is separated from its home and owner. If your veterinarian isn't able to help, he should refer you to a behaviorist

MISCHIEF AND MISBEHAVIOR

All puppies and even some adult dogs will get into mischief at some time in their lives. You should start by "puppy proofing" your house. Even so it is impossible to have a sterile environment. For instance, if you would be down to four walls and a floor your dog could still chew a hole in the wall. What do you do? Remember puppies should never be left unsupervised so let us go on to the trusted adult dog that has misbehaved. His behavior may be an attention getter. Dogs, and even children, are known to do mischief even though they know they will be punished. Your puppy/dog will benefit from more attention and new direction. He may benefit from a training class or by reinforcing the obedience he has already learned. How about a daily walk? That could be a good outlet for your dog, time together and exercise for both of you.

Suggested Reading

The Beagle
PS-811
Marcia Foy and Anna Katherine Nicholas
320 pages, photos throughout.

Owner's Guide to Dog Health
TS-214
Dr. Lowell Ackerman, DVM
432 pages, over 300 full-color photos.

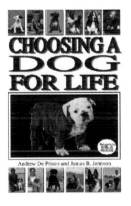

Skin and Coat Care For Your Dog
TS-249
Dr. Lowell Ackerman, DVM
224 pages, over 190 full-color photos.

Choosing A Dog For Life
TS-257
Andrew DePrisco
384 pages, over 700 full color photos.

159

INDEX